Praise for *Be a Gre Manager - Now!*

'A compact yet insightful book providing a wide range of practical aspects of management: ideas, explanations and examples. This book is useful to the seasoned manager as well as those novice intent on making themselves great managers.'
Junid Saham, Director, Master-Pack Group, Penang and Director, Areca Capital, Kuala Lumpur and former Director of Dialog Group Berhad, Kuala Lumpur

'Whether you are a millennial in management or embarking on management, you have to read this no nonsense, straight to the point book. It's a must-read.'
Chris Browne, Development and Employability Coach, Resident Coach on Sky TV's The Chrissy B Show

'An excellent book – one every manager should read if they want to succeed.'
Professor Ashley Braganza, Professor of Organisational Transformation and Head of Economics and Finance, Brunel University London

'A book to help you bridge the gap and understand the unwritten rules of management in order to develop the professional skill set to inspire and motivate your team to success.'
Katharine Lovell, Deputy Headteacher, Fearnhill School

'This book is packed full of little gems which will help managers at all levels be at their best. A must-read for anyone who is serious about management as a profession.'
Debbie Niven, Director and Co-founder of Momentum Training & Management Consultants

Be a Great Manager - Now!

The 2in1 Manager: Speed Read - instant
tips; Big Picture - lasting results

Audrey Tang

PEARSON

Harlow, England • London • New York • Boston • San Francisco • Toronto • Sydney
Auckland • Singapore • Hong Kong • Tokyo • Seoul • Taipei • New Delhi
Cape Town • São Paulo • Mexico City • Madrid • Amsterdam • Munich • Paris • Milan

Pearson Education Limited
Edinburgh Gate
Harlow CM20 2JE
United Kingdom
Tel: +44 (0)1279 623623
Web: www.pearson.com/uk

First published 2016 (print and electronic)

Pearson Education is not responsible for the content of third-party internet sites.

ISBN: 978-1-292-11966-3 (print)
        978-1-292-11968-7 (PDF)
        978-1-292-11969-4 (ePub)

British Library Cataloguing-in-Publication Data
A catalogue record for the print edition is available from the British Library

Library of Congress Cataloging-in-Publication Data
Names: Tang, Audrey, author.
Title: Be a great manager--now! : speed read--instant tips; big picture--lasting
    results / Audrey Tang.
Description: Harlow, United Kingdom : Pearson Education, [2016] | Series:
    Speed read | Includes bibliographical references and index.
Identifiers: LCCN 2016000778 (print) | LCCN 2016006267 (ebook) |
    ISBN 9781292119663 (pbk.) | ISBN 9781292119694 (e-pub)
Subjects: LCSH: Executives. | Executive ability. | Management.
Classification: LCC HD38.2 .T366 2016 (print) | LCC HD38.2 (ebook) | DDC
    658.4/09--dc23
LC record available at http://lccn.loc.gov/2016000778

10 9 8 7 6 5 4 3 2 1
20 19 18 17 16

Cover design by Two Associates

Print edition typeset in Scene Std 10/14 pts by SPi Global
Print edition printed in Great Britain by Henry Ling Ltd, at the Dorset Press, Dorchester, Dorset

NOTE THAT ANY PAGE CROSS REFERENCES REFER TO THE PRINT EDITION

Contents

About the author

Audrey attained her Doctorate from Brunel University Business School. Her thesis focused on the training and support of service professionals. She is trained as an executive coach and her academic background is psychology and law. Prior to training and coaching, Audrey was a secondary school drama teacher (QTS), later progressing to Programme Manager for vocational qualifications in 'Supporting Teaching and Learning', and 'Childcare, Learning and Development', within Further Education.

Audrey is the founder of CLICK Training Consultancy. CLICK specialises in experiential learning and offers CPD Standards accredited workshops on personal development and employability skills for university students, as well as soft-skills for new managers. Audrey currently writes and delivers CLICK's training programmes for universities, corporate and community clients. She is also a member of the HEA and the BPsS.

As well as appearing as the resident wellbeing expert for *The Chrissy B Show* (Sky 203), Audrey hosts *Lifestyle:MK* on Secklow Sounds Radio (105.5FM), Saturdays 12–2pm, and she regularly writes for and presents at national and international conferences within the field of learning and development.

Publisher's acknowledgements

We are grateful to the following for permission to reproduce copyright material:

Figures
Figure 3.1 from *Coaching for Performance,* 4 ed., Nicholas Brealey Publishing (John Whitmore 2009).

Picture Credits
The publisher would like to thank the following for their kind permission to reproduce their photographs:

(Key: b-bottom; c-centre; l-left; r-right; t-top)

Pearson Education Ltd: 123rf.com 11, 12, 43, 51, 54, 59, 71, 72, 93t, 108, 140b, 156, 157, 163, 176, 197, 201, 202t, 213, 219, 229, Africa Studio. 139r, Alexander Raths 178, ALMAGAMI 93, alphaspirit 84, 99, 210, 228, Anatolii Stoiko 137, Andresr. Shutterstock 39, Andrey Burmakin 162, Andy Dean Photography 216, Nagy-Bagoly Arpad 58, aslysun 150, auremar 81, 82, 180, Michael D Brown 31, Cartoonresource 40, Konstantin Chagin 45, Champion studio 102, Chatchawan 204, Stephen Coburn 24, 52, Stephen Coburn 24, 52, Creativa 13, Chris Curtis 5, Darq 8, Jeanette Dietl 15, Dmitriy Shironosov 112, donskarpo 206t, EdBockStock 76, EDHAR 64, Elena Larina 140t, Elena Yakusheva 110, Elnur 65, EmiliaUngur 205, estherpoon 38, g-stockstudio 183, Blaj Gabriel 131, Christos Georghiou 3, 79, 142, Gunnar Pippel 41, Hadi Djunaedi 165, Helder Ameida 109b, Hurst Photo 159, hxdbzxy 206b, iofoto 146, iQoncept 4, 91, 109t, 149, 171, 173, 207, Brian A Jackson 37, Junial Enterprises 174b, Kamil Macniak 119, Lasse Kristensen 190, Lightspring 75, Linda Bucklin. Shutterstock 225, Lindsay Lewis

Publisher's acknowledgements

74, Lisa S. 89, Lord and Leverett 195, mangostock 125, Marcin Balcerzak 174t, 186, mast3r 202b, mtkang 6, Novelo 73, Olaru Radian-Alexandru 221, ostill 172, PathDoc 21, Paul Vasarhelyi 114, Pearson Education, Inc. 90, 132, 141, Pressmaster 28, 107, Syda Productions 46, Rafal Olechowski 147, 226, Rawpixel 77, Rido 122, Risto Viita 7, Robert Churchill 113, S.john 61, Anirban Sarkar 9, Sean Locke Photography 175, Sergey Nivens 96, sharpshutter 193, spaxiax 22, stefanolunardi 128, Steve Collender 48, Stuart Miles 143, 209, sunsetman 139l, szefei 118, Tatiana Popova 203, Teerapun 153, Kheng Guan Toh 33, 116, Tom Davison 19, Vadym Drobot 196, Varina and Jay Patel 42, wavebreakmedia 18, YanLev 126, Yeko Photo Studio 139c, Zudy and Kysa 138, Zurijeta 111.

All other images © Pearson Education

Foreword

The landscape of management has changed, with social media in particular playing a large role in the shape of the business world. This is not just through growing global accessibility, but also through the way it changes the perceptions, and often the behaviour, of those who engage in it – which is (at the time of writing) approximately 1 in 4 people across the globe (eMarketer report, 2013).

Accessibility to so many things provides daily distraction, and human wants (and seemingly *needs*) are changing too. While, fundamentally, the management theories taught in business schools still hold true, they need to be modified to address these changes – at least in their practical application.

This book reminds managers of the foundation theories that they have been taught, while applying them in the context of the 'new world'. It seeks to assist with organisational 'fire-fighting' as well as to offer proactive ideas when something isn't your fault . . . but has become your problem.

It is not a regimented 'How To', but rather offers ideas, explanations and examples to give the new manager more pathways to action in an ever-demanding world.

References

eMarketer report (2013) Social networking reaches nearly one in four, *Emarketer.com*, http://www.emarketer.com/Article/Social-Networking-Reaches-Nearly-One-Four-Around-World/1009976 (retrieved September 2015).

Chapter 1

Think like a manager

1.1 The transit from 'involvement' to 'co-ordination'

The moment you take on a management role, your focus changes from 'doing the work' to 'getting the work done'. You have moved from being a team worker to the position of co-ordinator or shaper (Belbin, 1981), and so must your mind-set. The first few weeks are essential for reframing your outlook because it is at this point of the transition where your old role will seem much easier and more comfortable than your new one. Never forget that work continues despite your 'period of adjustment' so you need to make a positive impression while hitting the ground running. As with the implementation of any successful change, you need the commitment to see it through. One of the hardest tasks is learning to *direct,* effectively, the jobs that you might once have enjoyed doing because their completion and quality is still your success measure.

Do this
Look at your current 'to do' list. How much of it needs to be done by *you* and how much can you delegate to your team? Identify the points for delegation and delegate at least one. (This has the extra benefit of buying you a little time to settle in.)

1.2 Know your job

A new management role, or indeed any new role, is like joining a familiar game without knowing the rules. If you have moved up within the organisation, you have an idea of how to play, but it is essential to double check that you were doing it right in the first place. Familiarity with the policies, or Standard Operating Procedures (SOPs), will always help ensure your practice is appropriate, and these documents will also form the backbone to dealing effectively with any disputes or problems. However, if you see that behaviour within your organisation contradicts the official policies, unless there is a clear risk to health and safety, it may be beneficial to spend some time simply observing and then, if necessary, changing the SOP accordingly. After all, it might be the policy that needs modification, not the practice.

Do this

If you haven't already, set aside some time this week to familiarise yourself with the key organisational policies, e.g. Sickness; Discipline; Bullying & Harassment; Rewards, Benefits and Expenses; Training & Development.

1.3 Ask, don't assume (1)

Even if you were lucky enough to have a handover period, there will be things that the previous manager did not explain. Unless they are a 'Corporate psychopath' (Boddy et al., 2010), this is not deliberate. They do not *want* you to fail, it is just because some things are like second nature to them or because they genuinely did not realise you needed to know. Never assume that the person handing over the role has told you everything. It is as much up to you to ask, proactively, for anything else that you may need to function effectively and as quickly as possible. It is not that people do not want to say something – they may just not realise that they need to.

Do this

Make a list of all the things you wish you'd known when you started your last job. (Or make a list of all the things you wish your manager had known while in your last job!) If you STILL don't know the answers – ask someone!

1.4 The (un)social network

There have been many reports of people getting fired because of questionable social network postings, and it is not uncommon for companies to check your 'profiles' prior to interview. If you have uploaded a picture publicly, those are the reasonable consequences. As a manager you need to be even more wary, and this can mean restricting your posts, and even your audience. It is certainly no longer appropriate to be typing throwaway comments about who you like or don't like in the office, and the cryptic 'You'll never guess what happened at work . . .' status feeds will do little to reassure your team, nor will they earn you the trust of your CEO. While you do not necessarily have to block people, you may need to explain to your friends why your social network profile is changing. If they are *real* friends, they will understand, and support you.

Do this

Look at your social media presence and ask yourself if you would be happy for your bosses to see it. If necessary, start a new profile where you can manage your friends list, privacy and posts from the onset.

1.5 Managing change

There is an implicit survival belief that if something has been around for a long time, it is probably good – after all, it has survived that long. As such, the arrival of a new manager can be disconcerting for a team, especially if the previous manager has been there for some time, or there has been consistency in the inconsistency. If you have moved up within the department you may need to address the way that your team have seen you in the past, and how they will see you now. The departmental chatter will cover 'What is s/he going to be like?', 'What will s/he change?' and the really big question 'Will s/he get on with *me*?' If they do not already know you, the team themselves will probably run your name through a search engine to have a look at your social network profile(s). You need to put your team at ease as soon as you take your position at the helm.

Do this

Have you had a chat with your team that isn't a formal meeting? As long as you're not affecting their deadlines, schedule in some time for a tea break with them . . . bring cake! (Or fruit!)

1.6 Old vision, new perspective

Whether you have taken over a management position or been promoted into one, your perspective of the organisation will change. You are now responsible for others in your workplace, not just yourself. From a more extrinsically motivated approach, e.g. 'I work to live', as a manager you will be more strongly committed to achieving the organisational mission and goals. After all *this* has become your new success measure. Part of your goal is to drive organisational success through the achievements of your team. However, your team may not – and do not have to – observe the same commitment. People are motivated to take a job for many reasons – money, personal success, ambition – to provide for their families, to enjoy the life to which they are accustomed, to be able to perform skills they love . . . and so on. The theories of motivation (Maslow, Herzberg, McClelland etc.) saturate the pages of leadership textbooks. Remain mindful that very few of these reasons generate a commitment to the organisation. Most will motivate the member of staff to remain in work, but unless they develop a commitment to the organisation, they may take their skills away as other opportunities open up for them. The achievement of your organisational vision relies also on maintaining the skills set within your staff. This means recognising and developing their talent in order to retain them and continually improve their performance.

Do this

Identify your high achievers and those who seem to be struggling (or keeping their heads down). Find out what is available to help you develop or support them further.

1.7 Get proactive

If you no longer care about your job, that is the time to stop managing it. Of course, this will never happen to you: you are raring to go, ready to take on this exciting challenge that you put yourself up for and achieved! But we are sentient beings, and as such cannot help but be influenced or affected by each other. What you do and how you behave has an impact on those around you. Your influence can therefore be positive or negative, and so can that of your team. The advantage of being in the manager's role is that you are finally in a position of some power where you can do something to positively affect the workplace. Do not waste that opportunity. Instead of always reacting, try to be proactive in your decisions, seek out opportunities for organisational or employee development and growth, and take pride in broadening your own knowledge. Learn from others, read widely – see this position as only the beginning of your career rather than an endpoint. A proactive approach to work will also keep you motivated!

Do this

Write down where you see your role within the organisation in five years. List three things you can do to start that journey. Do one tomorrow!

BIG PICTURE
1. Think like a manager

1.1 The transit from 'involvement' to 'co-ordination'

> 'A manager is not a person who can do the work better than his men; he is a person who can get his men to do the work better than he can.'
>
> (Frederick W. Taylor, 1911)

Why

A common reason for moving into management or achieving promotion is because you are very good at the job you are currently doing. However, management requires a new skills set. You have to learn to communicate clearly so that your team understand exactly what is required of them; you might need to teach or support staff with tasks that you found easy; you may need to motivate people to complete duties you would have done for free. You will also have authority to make decisions or effect change, within organisational boundaries, and you may be faced with more reporting and feedback tasks which assist the smooth running of the department. You have become more

ur allegiance to your organisation's values and
ment is the task of developing others to perform
but just doing the job yourself. Of course your
anding of the work is important, but it will
improvement of working conditions, resources

Business brief

A common goal is promotion, but once this is achieved organisations do not always think, or know how, to develop staff within their new position. This results in poor performance and disillusioned managers. Roberts (1994) found that those who perform well within a job tend to be good managers – but they do require further training. With this in place to develop the management skills set, and options for those who preferred not to take a management route, organisational retention was higher than would be the case if one or both these factors were not present. While promotion is a goal, management is a *choice*, and only the beginning of a career path.

Try this

Congratulations on achieving your goal. Now focus on management as a new challenge:

1. Reflect on your strengths and weaknesses in relation to your new tasks.

2. Ask for help or for training to develop your skills. If this can be demonstrated via your Training Needs Analysis, the incentive will be all the greater. Why wait until your first appraisal to ask for support?

3. Recognise that your work relationships may need to change.

4. Understand the direction for your department or team's overall direction is and communicate this effectively.

5. Appreciate that while your perspective and goals will change, those of your team may not. With this in mind, find a way to collaborate with them to achieve your success measures.

. . . and if management is *not* for you, move onto what is!

Reflection

- How did it work?

- What will I do next time?

References

Belbin, M. (1981) *Management Teams.* London: Heinemann.

Roberts, K. (1994) The transition into management by scientists and engineers: A misallocation or efficient use of human resources? *Human Resource Management,* 33: 561–579.

Taylor, F.W. (1911) *The Principles of Scientific Management.* New York, NY and London: Harper & Brothers.

1.2 Know your job

> 'There is nothing which rots morale more quickly and more completely than . . . the feeling that those in authority do not know their own minds.'
>
> (Lionel Urwick, 1956)

Why

Obviously, knowing what you are doing is central to your credibility, and management also involves knowing what everyone in your team should be doing too. However, many managers find that a lack of knowledge of company policy has been the cause of their problems in dealing with issues such as sickness because staff members 'know the system', but they do not. If you know your systems, while you familiarise yourself with your day-to-day responsibilities you will also be able to acknowledge if anything needs to be changed – *and* be in a position to effect that change. Your new viewpoint enables you to determine whether it is the process that is inefficient or if the problem lies in the execution (as a team member it is easy to blame the former). To borrow a medical term, once a period of 'watchful waiting' has been completed you are more able to implement change because you have a better idea of what might be wrong, and a greater understanding of your team, enabling you to action the change with the least resistance.

Business brief

Neurolinguistic Programming (NLP) practitioners (and athletes) use the 'match, pace, lead' technique for success (O'Connor, 2013). This involves being able to match the person or situation (in the case of a transaction it may be the emotional nuance of the speaker; in sport it will be the race leader), then pace (i.e. move alongside) it before eventually leading it to its conclusion. The same process helps implement change effectively too. If you know the practices within your department and can function within them for a time so you get a clear understanding of how they, and the people who perform them, operate, it is then much easier to lead a change from that position compared with trying to instigate it cold.

Try this

In your new position, before implementing change:

1. Consider whether it is the practice that needs to be changed or the procedure that needs to be rewritten to accommodate the practice. Remain mindful that rewriting a policy can also be perceived as defeatist, e.g. 'If you can't beat 'em . . .', so be clear on your reasons, and be able to explain them.

2. Familiarise yourself with how your department runs – the written operational practices as well as what the team are doing as a matter of course – and work alongside them before leading your change.

3. Make sure you are aware of HR policies or Standard Operating Procedures need changing. This may involve time sequences that need to be updated, or evidential records from issues or events that may necessitate a change in procedure.

Reflection

- How did it work?

```

```

- What will I do next time?

```

```

References

O'Connor, J. (2013), *The NLP Workbook: Newburyport, MA:* Conari Press.

Urwick, L. (1956) The span of control, *Harvard Business Review,* May–June.

1.3 Ask, don't assume (1)

'Vice comes from bad habits and aiming at the wrong things, not deliberately . . .'

(Aristotle)

Why

Management, like most professional roles, does not afford a great deal of 'settling in' time. If you have clocked in and you are not wearing a training badge or 'L-plate', you are implying that you can do the job. Therefore it is part of your responsibility to gather as much information as you can to make it easy on yourself. When people are vacating a position, especially one they have held for some time, their focus is not necessarily on passing on the mantle. In addition, sometimes they do not realise how much their work has become habitual. You have the advantage of a fresh pair of eyes as well as the drive to succeed in this brand new opportunity, so a little bit of extra effort at this stage will serve you well.

Business brief

Research by MIT has found that habit takes over as practice progresses (Dougherty, 2015). Once something becomes habitual, you think about it less, which means it becomes more difficult to change or adapt. Be mindful of that in the practices of your predecessor. However, good practice is to form your own 'Things to do' practices for whenever you move into a new position. Look at the practices surrounding your role, and ask about anything that strikes you as odd.

NB: 'We've always done it that way' is not a good reason; see section 7.7.

Try this

Have a checklist of things that you need to ask at your induction. These might include:

1. Location of the HR policies.

2. Budget holder authorisation forms.

3. Other authorisation forms required (e.g. mileage claims, holiday, sickness, timesheets, insurance).

4. Appraisal and mandatory training records for the team.

5. How to access the intranet.

6. Names and contacts for specific departments (e.g. procurement, finance, HR, learning and development).

7. Fire procedure and any regular test dates.

8. Departmental practices (e.g. 'Pizza Fridays').

Reflection

- How did it work?

- What will I do next time?

References

Aristotle and Sachs, J. (2002) *Nicomachean Ethics.* Newbury, MA: Focus Publishing/R. Pullin.

Boddy, C., Ladyshewsky, R.K. and Galvin, P.G. (2010) Leaders without ethics in global business: corporate psychopaths, *Journal of Public Affairs,* 10, June, 121–138.

Dougherty, A. (2015) Neurons drive habit, *News.mit.edu,* 19 August, http://news.mit.edu/2015/neurons-drive-habit-0819 (retrieved September 2015).

1.4 The (un)social network

*'We don't have a choice on **whether** we do social media. The question is how **well** we do it.'*

(Qualman, 2010)

Why

We are all using social media, and so are our customers, clients and colleagues. It is a means of building a network, targeting a wider reach than conventional media methods, but also a form of self-expression. However, while writer Pearl S. Buck (1954) wrote about self-expression being a form of expressing one's feelings, personality or ideas through art, the term has taken on a wider definition, e.g. the posting of a timeline of your life on a forum where online 'friends' are invited to pass judgment. Because social network profiles are so commonplace, it is important to maintain an awareness that they need to be managed correctly. If you would not say something in public, why would you feel more comfortable writing it and pressing 'send'? The perceived distance between yourself and your audience is deceptive. While you might have written something in the privacy of your bedroom, someone has accessed it in the privacy of theirs – you have not only connected directly with them, but you have done so in what would ordinarily have been an intimate setting. If you are not prepared to interact in that way with your colleagues in real life, you should certainly not be doing so online.

Business brief

Eurocom Worldwide (2012) conducted a survey of employer behaviour with regard to social networks and found that one in five bosses have rejected an applicant on account of their social network profile. The previous year they reported that almost 40% of companies who responded said that they would look at an applicant's social network profile prior to inviting them to interview. However, a survey by CareerBuilder found that while candidates were being rejected or reprimanded for social network profiles which included poor grammar and spelling as well as inappropriate posts or photographs, well-managed profiles contributed to candidates landing promotions or dream jobs. The common reasons cited by CareerBuilder (2012) for hiring a candidate based on their social network profile were:

- The candidate appeared a good fit for the company culture
- The candidate showed a wide range of interests
- The candidate's profile was creative.

Try this

1. Update your privacy settings and, if necessary, limit the audience for information you choose to post on social media.

2. Update settings so that you need to review 'tagged' posts (while you may not be able to restrict someone else from posting something embarrassing, you certainly do not need to link it to your own network).

3. Ask people to remove photographs of you that you do not want to be made public – or at the very least to 'cut you out' prior to posting them.

4. Make sure that anything that will be broadcast publicly is something you are happy to be seen by anyone worldwide. Once it is out of your control, *anything* can happen to it.

5. Update your site to convey the sort of image you would want to see of a manager.

Reflection

- How did it work?

- What will I do next time?

References

Buck, P.S. (1954) *My Several Worlds: A Personal Record.* New York, NY: John Day.

CareerBuilder (2012) www.CareerBuilder.co.uk (retrieved July 2015).

Eurocom Worldwide Survey (2012) www.eurocompr.com/prfitem. asp?id=14921 (retrieved December 2015).

Qualman, E. (2010) *Socialnomics.* New York, NY: Wiley.

1.5 Managing change

> *'Every success story is a tale of constant adaptation, revision and change. A company that stands still will soon be forgotten.'*
>
> (Richard Branson, 2015)

Why

> *'One of the reasons "change" is difficult is because " ... the longer something is thought to exist, the better it is evaluated".'*
>
> (Eidelman et al., 2010)

Your arrival as a new manager is the first change that your team will need to become accustomed to, so it needs to be handled sensitively. After all, the way you manage your arrival speaks volumes about the way you will manage the rest of your work. Managers need to be people focused as much as task focused, and the most successful manager will encourage their team to

collaborate with, not compromise for, them (Blake and Mouton, 1964). This collaboration becomes essential as you progress through your managerial life. When your team share a common goal, everyone pulls together to attain it. This becomes its own reward.

Business brief

Any change is made easier by collaboration, and to encourage this, you need to build trust. Ricci and Wiese (2011) suggest that poor collaboration is worse than no collaboration at all, and stress the importance of building trust between colleagues. Such trust begins with the manager, and progresses into the team as a whole as they commit to shared organisational goals and so reap the rewards. It is not a straightforward task and needs a manager who is able to communicate, who works with integrity and who *follows through on their commitments or promises.* However, as always, good practice can become habitual. By smoothly managing your arrival as the first change your team have to face, the groundwork will be laid to affect future change successfully.

Try this

1. Do not expect everyone to like you right away. In fact do not expect everyone to like you ever . . . the main thing is that they trust you and will work for you.

2. Find a time to meet with the department as a whole to introduce yourself, as well as meeting with the individual members of the team. This is a good chance to hear their aspirations within the organisation so that you can continue to develop them.

3. If you have worked within the team before acknowledge that your new role may seem a little strange at first for all concerned.

4. Even if change needs to be implemented quickly, try not to do it straight away. Remember what you learned in section 1.2: take a moment to learn the ropes, then you can Match, Pace and Lead.

5. If you are there to head a restructure, do not lull people into a false sense of security. Being honest (within your remit) and giving them time to prepare for change can be beneficial for the well-being of the team.

6. Understand that people will become accustomed to change at different times. Make sure that you remain professional and consistent with your words and actions.

7. Learn from your own experiences with managers – which behaviours worked for you, which did not?

8. When you need to implement a change that has been fed down to you, if you are unsure, then ask about the reasoning behind it, and, as long as you are not breaching confidentiality, you will then be able to give a summary to your team. When people understand the reasons behind a change they are better able to deal with it.

9. Always be clear with your communications – your message is only as good as how well it is received.

10. If you have made a promise, stick to it.

11. Try NOT to make promises (things often change very fast in business)!

Reflection

- How did it work?

What will I do next time?

References

Blake, R. and Mouton, J. (1964). *The Managerial Grid: The Key to Leadership Excellence.* Houston, TX: Gulf Publishing Co.

Branson, R. (2015) *My Top 10 Quotes on Change,* Virgin.com, http://www.virgin.com/richard-branson/my-top-10-quotes-on-change (retrieved August 2015).

Eidelman, S., Pattershall, J. and Crandall, C.S. (2010) Longer is better, *Journal of Experimental Social Psychology,* 46(6), 9930998.

Ricci, R. and Wiese, C. (2011) *The Collaboration Imperative.* San Jose, CA: Cisco Systems.

1.6 Old vision, new perspective

'Once you realise that you're in something that you've always wanted and you don't want to lose it, you behave differently . . . and that means the integrity, the professionalism, and knowing what's right from wrong.'

(Paul Anka, 2013)

Why

In a small organisation it is sometimes possible to hire only the staff who are as committed as you to the success of your organisation. This is often true of start-ups where people may need to work voluntarily for some time. In a larger organisation, your team may have chosen to work there for many reasons including 'It's better than nothing', 'I can't get a job anywhere else' and 'I'm just biding my time until I retire.' This does not necessarily mean that they will under-perform, but it does mean that you need to first motivate them to find pleasure in personal success with which they can associate. While a member of your team may not care whether the organisation turns a profit or wins an award at the end of the year, they will feel a sense of reward if their personal contribution is acknowledged. This will be a factor when considering if they should move elsewhere – it was probably a factor for you too at some point. In a sideways move, people tend to be leaving their manager, rather than their job, so make sure they do not leave you. You are now committed to the organisation, so try and get

your team to commit to you and in turn your organisation will develop. Your actions will speak for the organisation. If you want people to commit to it, get them to commit to you first.

Business brief

Do not expect all employees to be as connected to the organisation as you. Instead, see yourself as the bridge between the organisation and your team. If you want the organisation to succeed, you must help your team to succeed – and retain the skills set. A Gallup Poll survey taken in 2006 found that for over one million US employees, 'a bad boss or supervisor' was the number one reason for leaving a job, and 75% of the reasons for employees leaving are related in some way to the manager (Robinson, 2008). Gallup further found that if employees felt 'connected to the organisation', this would be a reason to stay. If there is not full commitment to helping the organisation succeed, retention and performance (and thus an organisational connection) can be improved by adequate investment in staff, such as training and development programmes (Vanthournout et al., 2006). A corporate social responsibility White Paper (Gross, 2009) also found that employee engagement was enhanced by positive community or ethical connections (see also section 7.4).

Try this

1. Familiarise yourself with the organisational mission, values, goals and development plan. (Forewarned is forearmed with regard to any planned restructuring or redundancies, and will help you treat your team with respect and integrity.)

2. Seek to find ways to develop your best employees and support those who are doing less well.

3. Maintain your own sense of integrity, ethics and corporate social responsibility (CSR), and be aware of (and highlight to your team) what your organisation does regarding CSR.

4. Remember how you felt when you were praised or ignored by your own manager. Use those experiences to be the manager you always wanted.

Reflection

- How did it work?

- What will I do next time?

References

Anka, P. (2013) Paul Anka talks learning right from wrong, *The Toronto Sun,* 15 April, http://www.torontosun.com/2013/04/15/paul-anka-talks-learning-right-from-wrong (retrieved August 2015).

Gross, R. (2009) Corporate social responsibility and employee engagement: making the connection [White Paper]. Available at http://www.mandrake.ca/bill/images/corporate_responsibility_white_paper.pdf (retrieved August 2015).

Robinson, J. (2008) Turning around your turnover problem. Gallup.com. www.gallup.com/businessjournal/106912/turning-around-your-turnover-problem.aspx (retrieved December 2015).

Vanthournout, D., Olson, K., Ceisel, J., White, A., Waddington, T., Barfield, T., Desai, S. and Mindrum, C. (2006) *Return on Learning: Training for High Performance at Accenture.* Chicago, IL: Agate B2.

1.7 Get proactive

'Being proactive is the foundation of the other habits of highly effective people.'

(Stephen Covey, 1989)

Why

Sharma (2006) advised that while it is not essential for everyone to think like a CEO, the most successful organisational cultures are ones where everyone is proactive. As social creatures, humans are conditioned to learn from others – especially those whom they perceive as being more knowledgeable or powerful (Bandura, 1963), so it is not uncommon for teams to take on the characteristics of their manager. Being proactive will enable you to contribute to driving the organisation forward in a direction that you want, as well as keeping you motivated and interested in your job. Proactivity affords an element of choice and control, another basic human need, which in turn can increase job satisfaction. If you demonstrate proactivity yourself, it is even easier for your team to be enthusiastic and follow your example.

Business brief

Rotter's Locus of Control personality framework (1954) found that individuals who believed that they had little control over their lives (i.e. who had an 'external locus of control') were more prone to clinical depression that those who believed they had some influence (i.e. an 'internal locus of control'). Within the workplace, it was found that employees who had more perceived control would be more proactive in improving conditions for themselves – or finding another job – compared to those with an external locus who tended to complain rather than act (Allen et al., 2005). While it seems counter-intuitive to want people to actively seek other employment, it is important to appreciate that your skilled and proactive staff *are* highly employable, and therefore are also worth actively retaining. A high-flying executive will want to be associated with a high-flying organisation and through a commitment to staff empowerment you are able not only to help grow your organisation, but to do so in a way that your high fliers will appreciate.

Try this

1. Make time for yourself – proactive thinking benefits from reflection, so try not to overfill your calendar every day. The manager who does this is likely to be reacting only, and this needs to change.

2. Make a commitment to your own CPD (Continuing Professional Development) – embrace all opportunities to learn. Even the annual mandatory training refresher might bring you a new way of doing something, or a method to remember *not* to use.

3. Use online networking platforms to make new connections with organisations or people that you might wish to collaborate with in the future.

4. On a smaller scale, learn to observe and interpret the climate within your department and try to anticipate any

issues while they are saplings before they take root and grow.

5. Accept that management will always be a challenge, but one that can continually enthuse and energise you once you are able to, well, manage it.

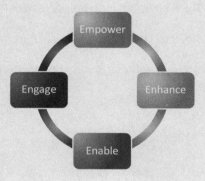

Reflection

- How did it work?

- What will I do next time?

References

Allen, D.G., Weeks, K.P. and Moffat, K.R. (2005) Turnover intentions and voluntary turnover: the moderating roles of self-monitoring, locus of control, proactive personality and risk aversion, *Journal of Applied Psychology,* 90, 980–990.

Bandura, A. (1963) *Social Learning and Personality Development.* New York, NY: Holt, Rinehart, and Winston.

Covey, S.R. (1989) *Seven Habits of Highly Effective People.* New York, NY: Free Press.

Rotter, J.B. (1954) *Social Learning and Clinical Psychology.* New York, NY: Prentice-Hall.

Sharma, R. (2006) *The Greatness Guide.* London: HarperElement.

Chapter 2

Making teams work

2.1 Know what a team is

A team is formed for the purpose of *getting a task done*. Whether you are choosing that team yourself or you are coming to a team that is already formed, people are there predominantly to play their part in the bigger picture, albeit for personal reasons. Therefore it is the bigger picture that needs to drive the team. If you lose sight of that picture, or do not know what it is, you soon lose sight of your team.

In the workplace the commonality is work and the organisation. While it is possible to meet people with whom you connect, this is not the essence of a workplace team. Teams that let their personal emotions overtake their focus are more likely to fall apart than those who retain the success of the task, project or organisation as the goal.

When respect predominates over liking, teams perform their jobs well – acknowledging other's contributions and appreciating differences in approach. Successful team players show awareness of their personal preferences, needs and shortcomings, but have the interpersonal skills that enable them to collaborate in order to attain the organisational goal – *and happy teams see, and experience, the value in doing so.*

Your role as a manager is first and foremost to ensure that *organisational success* is what motivates everyone in your team to the point where individual differences are accepted and recognised as the way to achieve.

But when will the success of the organisation motivate your team? When the rewards that fall from that success (over which you have some control) have a direct impact on their personal needs, e.g. investment in the working environment, a bonus, job security, promotion, working with people they like or praise.

Do this

Identify the bigger picture of your department. Are your team motivated to achieve it? Identify what will inspire them by reflecting on each individual.

2.2 Know your team

When leading a new team, it is important that you know who your team are as regards their workplace behaviours. This is where training tools such as the MBTI®, Belbin®, Merrill-Reid or other inventories can be helpful. Not only will you be able to identify the type of work your team may enjoy and do well, but you will also gain insight into their communication style and how best to instruct and motivate them.

In rewarding your team, consider what brought them to work for your organisation in the first instance. Remember it is the achievement of the organisational goal (*and how that achievement also fulfils your team's personal needs*) that can make the incidental personal gripes or frustrations worth the effort. Do not forget, however, that goals and motivations are fluid. Always be mindful that over time your team's personal and work needs and preferences may change.

Do this

Find out if your organisation offers a 'team tool' such as the MBTI®, or Belbin®.

2.3 Right person right task

Just because someone can do something doesn't mean they are the best person for the job. All too often a task is assigned to a team member because experience has shown they are good at it. However, part of your role is to *develop* your staff. Your investment means that they, and your department, can continue to grow within a fast-changing business world.

Do not view work as a static entity. Every organisation needs to keep moving forward. In the competitive business world your organisation does not just stagnate, it starts falling behind. The

tasks that your team are currently doing may not be the same ones that they will be expected to do 12 months from now. History teaches us that specialisation, no matter how perfect the product, is no guarantee of continuation. Too narrow a speciality can mean that when that task is made redundant, so too is the worker. Make sure your best workers want, *and are able*, to remain with you!

Do this

Find out what your organisation's three- to five-year goal is. Ask yourself: will my department cope? List three ways you can start making your team development-ready right now.

2.4 Dealing with disputes and problems

As well as pre-empting and addressing the potential disputes and problems that may arise within a team, it is important to acknowledge the role your team themselves have to play. In the most effective teams, disputes and problems are dealt with at ground level. If your team are confident, capable and have the perceived authority to address their issues, they will tend to do so, which is very empowering.

Escalating an issue can be perceived as a sign of weakness. However, it may also be done with an air of 'I'm not paid enough

"Aren't you glad we had this meeting to resolve our conflict?"

to deal with this'. Either way, if you are dealing with a dispute or problem that has been brought to your attention you are required not only to address the problem, but also to address why it happened and how to avoid it in future. The latter two points may highlight an issue within your organisation, or your management, that needs to be addressed. If you do not mend the root cause, the problem will recur.

Do this

Think of the last dispute settled in your organisation. Was the root cause addressed? If so, keep it at the back of your mind as a model when you need to do the same. (If not, make a note of how you will behave differently.)

2.5 Challenging perceived favouritism or discrimination

While you may have understandable reasons for treating one of your team differently from another, the charge of favouritism can still be levied at you, which in turn creates discord within your team. As humans we all have personal preferences, and likes and dislikes. We have a tendency to prefer situations and people that we understand or make us feel comfortable. As such, it is easy to overlook favouritism or discrimination in yourself, as you are just doing what makes you comfortable or avoiding what makes

you uncomfortable. However, adherence to the policies and procedures will avoid both favouritism and discrimination – when our own emotions blur the lines.

Do this

Reflect on your actions from today. How might they have been perceived by an outside observer?

2.6 360° feedback for all

Appraisals are often mistrusted within organisations as they are seen as a 'tick box' exercise, yet, when done well, they can offer valuable insights into current performance and ways of improving. One of the appraisal methods you may already be using is 360° feedback. If you involve your team in your own appraisal process, you not only have a means to develop yourself, but you will have also started to embed a culture of appraisal.

If you do not trust the appraisal method, why should your team?

Do this

List the positives that can come out of appraisals – convey these to your team . . . then ask them to appraise you.

2.7 There is a 'me' in team

Management affords you the opportunity to make a difference. It is only in this capacity that you have the authority to effect change. Departmental and personal growth are as important as each other. The more skills your team attain, the further they can take the department, which in turn may yield more personal achievements for them.

ORGANISATIONAL SUCCESS -> PERSONAL REWARDS -> HAPPY TEAM

As a manager you need to encourage cohesiveness, but also enable each individual to grow at their own pace. This means they have to learn through making their own mistakes and generating their own solutions. Of course, you may be time-bound so direct input may be necessary at times, but if you have selected the right person for the job, and allowed enough time for support as required, it is best to turn your attention to progressing your own role.

Do this

Identify one thing that makes each member of your team individual in their contribution. Praise them for it.
Then praise yourself.

2.1 Know what a team is

> 'Teamwork is the ability to work together toward a common vision. The ability to direct individual accomplishments toward organisational objectives.'
>
> (Andrew Carnegie, cited in Ventura and Templin, 2005)

Why

A common desire of new managers (even if they don't admit it out loud) is to have the sort of team portrayed in TV dramas – a group of contradictory, yet complementary, people who pull together into the family you choose for yourself. This is idealistic, although not impossible. Your priority needs to be not on the group, but on the task and the working environment.

You will never please everyone because the emotions of other people are not under your control. However, you do have control over the working environment, the work you delegate and the rewards and recognition you give, which all contribute to the overall atmosphere. In the same way as customer loyalty correlates with customer experience (Shaw, 2007), so too can

team loyalty, productivity and performance be generated by a positive workplace experience.

Business brief

A team is 'a group in which members work together intensively to achieve a common group goal' (Shapiro, 2002). It is not necessary for the team to enjoy each other's company as long as there is respect for each other's skills, clear and open communication, and a positive work ethic to achieve the goal. If the goal then results in individual personal needs being met, you will find that the team operates well on a personal level too.

Your task in a managing a team is to ensure that everyone understands and respects each other's role, that your team have the skills (interpersonal and otherwise) to achieve the task and that the achievement of the goal is meaningful.

Try this

1. Be aware of the organisation's five-year plan and how it will benefit your team.

2. Communicate this to your team so that it is a shared vision.

3. Make sure each team member understands the importance of their role and that of each other in achieving the shared vision.

4. Ensure your team have the skills (interpersonal and practical) to do the tasks you require, and provide training if they don't.

5. Be aware of what motivates your team personally, and tailor your rewards (where possible) to those motivations.

6. Remember that you cannot make people like each other, but you can achieve a positive working environment by attending to the above.

Reflection

- How did it work?

- What will I do next time?

References

Coyle-Shapiro, J.A. (2002) A psychological contract perspective on organizational citizenship behavior. *Journal of Organizational Behavior,* 23(8), 927–946.

Shaw, C. (2007) *The DNA of Customer Experience: How Emotions Drive Value.* Basingstoke: Palgrave MacMillan.

Ventura, S. and Templin, M.C. (2005) *Five Star Teamwork: How to Achieve Success . . . Together.* Bedford, TX: Walk the Talk Company.

2.2 Know your team

'Strength lies in differences, not in similarities.'

(Stephen Covey, 2004)

Why

The knowledge that personality inventories such as the MBTI®, Merrill-Reid and Belbin® (to name only a few) provide information that is helpful in identifying your team's communication preferences, what positions within the group they enjoy and how they are best motivated. This is not new. The right person in the right place enhances productivity and performance. Also not new is the awareness that in spite of their preferences regarding their working environment, people's motivation to work at all is personal and individual. However many managers are unable to work effectively with the information that they gather, and also do not realise that those preferences, motivations and desired rewards change over time.

Business brief

While personality inventories give you information about the individuals within your team, and give your team an insight into why they think as they do, their use can either be an expensive exercise where a simple 'Buzzfeed Quiz' (Grandioni, 2014) would have worked instead, or an investment resulting in new management styles and a team who is now empowered to take active control over their choices.

The results of your inventory of choice need to be used to effect better communication within your team, improved leadership and breaking down of silos. This means listening to what their needs and issues are – and getting others to listen too – then acting on the information you have.

However, do not do this in isolation; instead, be aware that departmental and personal growth needs to fit within the organisational vision.

Try this

1. If you are holding a 'listening event' be sure to also ask for solutions. Not only is this good practice for your team but they will also find it empowering.

2. Require honesty from your team and ensure they feel able to speak their mind.

3. Try taking a 'matrix' approach to your team:

List your team members and their inventory results. Then ask them to list the issues that they currently have or have raised in the past, e.g.

Name	MBTI	Issues raised	Action needed	Opportunities for growth	Reflection
Sally Smith	ESFP	Feels undervalued			
Joe Bloggs	INTJ	Team feels that he could contribute more in meetings			

> Ask them to generate possible solutions as well as identifying opportunities for development that they would like to pursue.
>
> Develop an action plan from each with SMART objectives.
>
> 4. Once your plan has been put into action, be aware of any issues that arise. This may indicate that your team's outlook has changed and that you need to revise your matrix.

Reflection

- How did it work?

- What will I do next time?

References

Belbin Team Roles Inventory: The Home of Belbin Team Roles, http://www.belbin.com/ (retrieved July 2015).

Buzzfeed Quizzes: http://www.buzzfeed.com/?country=uk (retrieved July 2015).

Covey, S.R. (2004) *The 7 Habits of Highly Effective People: Restoring the Character Ethic*. New York, NY: Free Press.

Doran, G.T. (1981) There's a S.M.A.R.T. way to write management's goals and objectives, *Management Review* (AMA FORUM), 70(11), 35–36.

Grandioni, D. (2014) Buzzfeed quizzes – how do they work? *The Huffington Post,* 20 February, http://www.huffingtonpost. com/2014/02/20/buzzfeed-quiz-how-do-they-work_n_4810992. html (retrieved September 2015).

MBTI®: The Myers & Briggs Foundation, http://www.myersbriggs. org/my-mbti-personality-type/mbti-basics/ (retrieved July 2015).

Merrill-Reid social styles inventory: Merrill, D.W. and Reid, R.H. (1999) *Personal Styles and Effective Performance.* New York, NY: CRC Press.

2.3 Right person right task

'Please, please, please – I would love to do some comedy. Once you have a reputation for one thing – in my case crying and dying – you are typecast.'

(Emily Watson, 2012)

Why

In practical terms, repetitive strain injury (RSI) is caused by 'doing a particular activity repeatedly or for a long period of time' (NHS Choices, 2015). Mentally, too, doing the same thing over and over again can result in burnout (Adams, 2011). However, employees often find an irony in the fact that the better they are at one particular task, the more they are called upon to do it.

This action makes short-term managerial sense. You want a task completed well, so you assign it to your best person. However,

praise or rewards for achieving that task may also begin to feel habitual rather than motivating. Ensure you are always developing your team, or else even 'sideways moves' become more attractive!

Business brief

MacGregor's Theory Y (1966) suggests that people are happy to work because they find fulfilment through making a contribution and gain a sense of achievement through using and developing their skills. Your tasks will continue to be carried out with a consistent level of quality if you continually develop the person you have assigned to do them. They will then be able to mentor new people in carrying out the same tasks, while developing the new skill of mentoring. If, throughout their professional lives, their work offers them a challenge, their approach will remain fresh.

Try this

1. If you can spare staff, having your 'expert' mentor a less experienced team member means that you have options in future task assignment. Further, you will then be able to develop your 'expert' as a mentor as well as freeing them up to do something different next time, in turn developing their skills.

2. While praise may be old hat to your 'expert', explain to them why they have been assigned that particular task again, and ask them what skills they would like to develop next time.

3. Ensure you look for and implement opportunities to develop your team.

4. Use Training Needs Analysis (TNA) to build up a skills profile of your team:

Name	TNA skills	New skills acquired	Possible development

Reflection

- How did it work?

- What will I do next time?

References

Adams, S. (2011) Boring jobs lead to burnout, *The Telegraph,* 26 June, http://www.telegraph.co.uk/news/health/8599684/Boring-jobs-lead-to-burn-out.html (retrieved July 2015).

Gordon, J. (2012) Emily Watson, why the actress signed her latest role, *The Daily Mail,* 9 January, http://www.dailymail.co.uk/home/you/article-2081772/Emily-Watson-Why-actress-signed-latest-role.html (retrieved August 2015).

McGregor, D. (1966) *The Human Side of Enterprise.* New York, NY: McGraw-Hill.

NHS Choices (2015) *Repetitive Strain Injury,* NHS Choices Website, http://www.nhs.uk/Conditions/Repetitive-strain-injury/Pages/Introduction.aspx (retrieved July 2015).

2.4 Dealing with disputes and problems

'Do not hover always on the surface of things . . . penetrate into the depth of matters, as far as your time and circumstances allow, especially in those things which relate to your profession.'

(Isaac Watts, 2010)

Why

There will always be disputes, and in the first instance you may do well to remind your team that the goal is the completion of the task. However, a positive working environment will always enhance performance, because energy and focus are not dissipated on gripes about other staff members. If you notice a dispute, or a team member brings one to your attention, then dealing with it

openly, although sensitively, is a priority before it takes more than a difficult conversation to resolve it. It is important to remember that if something has been escalated to the point where you are made aware, you not only need to fix it, but you must also prevent it from happening in future. This means getting to the root cause of the problem.

Business brief

Lencioni (2002) identified five key ways in which teams can be dysfunctional. He claimed that they can (i) lack attention to results; (ii) lack accountability; (iii) lack commitment; (iv) fear conflict; and (v) lack trust. In addition, the perception of these dysfunctions can be as damaging as the reality.

If a dispute or problem comes to your attention that pertains to you, first of all consider whether you are guilty of any of the above, or if you may have been perceived as such. The power of a psychological contract is such that any breach can result in increased staff turnover and certainly lowered productivity (Conway and Briner, 2005). If you have made a promise that you have not kept, especially without explanation, or if you have created a climate of mistrust or lack of appreciation through your behaviour, even if unintentionally, you must address the problem and take steps to resolve it.

However, if the dispute or problem is unrelated to you, remember that the person who has escalated it may feel disempowered, because they have had to hand control to someone else, or may feel they have no authority to control the situation. In fixing the problem it is also important *to fix the process so that the same situation does not recur,* and to ensure that power (and perhaps authority) is handed back to the person who escalated the issue in the first instance.

The 'root' is often a manifestation of one or more of the five dysfunctions being played out on the business stage. Investigate the potential causes of the problem and take steps at the root to avoid its recurrence. Check if your team's behaviour is causing any of the five dysfunctions, and identify what skills, knowledge or authority the team needs in order to resolve the issue for themselves in future.

Try this

1. Make a note of the disputes or problems that are escalated as this may bring you to a larger organisational problem that needs addressing. If this is the case, make sure you deal with it at the root – or at least bring it to the attention of your own managers.

2. Make a note of why the person who escalated the dispute or problem was unable to deal with it themselves, and identify what knowledge, skills or authority they would need in order to deal with it next time.

3. Furnish them with the knowledge, skills or authority they need to deal with it next time – and do not forget to praise them if they did all they could do prior to escalation.

4. Monitor the situation for any recurrence.

5. It is even possible to use this basic checklist for disputes or problems that you feel unable to deal with.

Reflection

- How did it work?

- What will I do next time?

┌───┐
│   │
│   │
│   │
│   │
│   │
└───┘

References

Conway, N. and Briner, R.B. (2005) *Understanding Psychological Contracts at Work: A Critical Evaluation of Theory and Research.* Oxford: Oxford University Press.

Lencioni, P.M. (2002) *The Five Dysfunctions of a Team: A Leadership Fable.* Chichester: John Wiley & Sons.

Watts, I. (2010) *The Improvement of the Mind; or, a Supplement to the Art of Logic in Two Parts,* by Isaac Watts, D.D. Also his Posthumous Works, Published from His Manuscript, by D Jennings, D.D. and P. Doddridge, D.D. Gale Ecco, Print Editions.

2.5 Challenging perceived favouritism or discrimination

'Even Jesus had a favourite.'

(Stephen Asma, 2012)

Why

Favouritism, and its counterpart, discrimination, merit a section to themselves because they are very easy to engage in these behaviours without realising.

Perceived favouritism, indeed any perceived inequity, can lead to disharmony within the team. This takes its greatest toll on channels of communication because those who feel out of favour may start deliberately communicating behind your back or withholding information, not maliciously but because it has

become a matter of habit. Not only will this have a negative effect on productivity, but it can also result in key team members leaving because of the working 'vibe'.

Business brief

Despite the laws against explicit discrimination, prejudices may be held implicitly and be expressed unconsciously. Fiske and Taylor (1991) said that humans are 'cognitive misers'. In order to achieve efficiency with our thought processes, we compartmentalise people. Prejudices and, in their lesser form, stereotypes, help us to do this. While you may feel more sympathetic to the plight of one team member than to that of another, you risk showing both favouritism and discrimination – not necessarily with regard to their race or gender, but perhaps to their work ethic, attitude, personality traits or something less discernible. While you may call it 'discretion' this behaviour can become very wrong.

Try this

1. Explain that while you are sympathetic, it would be unfair to the rest of the team to act contrary to the policy guidelines.

2. Be aware of your relationships and responses to your team. If you have a more positive or negative feeling towards one rather than another, you are at risk of demonstrating favouritism (or discrimination) at some point.

3. Try to keep your judgment as objective as possible – evidence helps. If you are managing people with whom you have a relationship outside of work, always support your decisions with substantiated facts.

4. If you do feel that you favour one of your team over another (or that you might be discriminating against one in particular), reflect on why this is the case. If it is something that can be changed, e.g. their work ethic, then meet with them and discuss what you would like to see happen. If this does not work, instigate proceedings in accordance with your policies (although you may first wish to seek advice from another manager to verify that you are not acting on prejudice).

Reflection

- How did it work?

- What will I do next time?

```



```

References

Asma, S.T. (2012) *Against Fairness.* Chicago, IL: University of Chicago Press.

Fiske, S.T. and Taylor, S.E. (1991) *Social Cognition,* 2nd edn. New York, NY: McGraw-Hill.

2.6 360° feedback for all

'Behaviour is the mirror in which everyone shows their image.'
(Johann Wolfgang von Goethe, cited in Corica, 2014)

Why

Appraisals are an excellent way to acknowledge the achievements of your team, as well as find out what their development goals are. They are also a good time to address, informally at first, any issues that may cause later problems at work. Appraisals are a great reason to collate a profile of evidence which may assist your team in achieving other steps within their career. For some professionals such as doctors who need to re-register their professional status after a specific time period, such a portfolio is essential. However, many – if not all – of your team will not see things that way. While appraisals are an opportunity to give and receive praise (the clue is in the title!), employees often fear criticism and perceive it as negative feedback rather than an opportunity to develop.

If you don't trust the system yourself then take steps to change it. A 'tick box' exercise is a waste of everyone's time.

If you believe in the appraisal process, demonstrate it by immersing yourself in it with your team. Let them see first-hand how you are able to learn and develop from their critique, but also how you appreciate their praise.

Business brief

The Washington Post (McGregor, 2014) published a study by Kansas State University which found that 'basically everybody hates performance reviews (appraisals)'. Culbertson et al. (2013) said this was true, even of people who 'enjoyed learning'. Even praise was described as 'relative' – with employees who worked hard 'being disappointed with a 4 rating instead of a 5'. Yet appraisals are still a staple of organisational practice.

Without any form of benchmark, progress becomes impossible to measure and praise becomes meaningless. Therefore unless another form of performance review can be developed, appraisals are here to stay. In reality, when done well, they become more than a star rating. In the same way as children have to be taught to look beyond their grade so, too, do your team.

Social Learning Theory (Bandura, 1977) is one of the most effective forms of learning. If your team see you embrace your appraisal and learn from it, they in turn will be less cynical, and may even look forward to their own.

Try this

1. Explain the reasoning behind the appraisal process.

2. Explain the importance of the appraisal process *not* being a 'tick box' or 'grading' exercise.

3. Encourage your team to be honest in their appraisal of you.

4. Encourage your team to ask others for feedback and consider it alongside their own views.

5. Encourage your team to always support their comments with evidence. (This also establishes good appraisal practice, and gathering evidence is helpful for demonstrating professional development too.)

6. Demonstrate your learning from the criticism as well as your appreciation of the praise.

7. Ask your team to reflect on the exercise and how this will assist their own appraisal preparation.

Reflection

- How did it work?

- What will I do next time?

┌───┐
│   │
│   │
│   │
│   │
│   │
│   │
│   │
└───┘

References

Bandura, A. (1977) *Social Learning Theory.* Englewood Cliffs, NJ: Prentice Hall.

Corica, L. (2014) *Making Changes Easily.* Bloomington, IN: Balboa Press.

Culbertson S.S., Henning, J.B. and Payne, S.C. (2013) Performance appraisal satisfaction: the role of feedback and goal orientation, *Journal of Personnel Psychology,* 12(4), 189–195.

McGregor, J. (2014) Every single person hates performance reviews, *The Washington Post,* 27 January, http://www.washingtonpost.com/blogs/on-leadership/wp/2014/01/27/study-finds-that-basically-every-single-person-hates-performance-reviews/ (retrieved July 2015).

2.7 There is a 'me' in team

'If you ever find a man who is better than you are – hire him. If necessary, pay him more than you pay yourself.'

(David Ogilvy, 2012)

Why

Your role in managing your team is first and foremost one of development rather than direct participation. Of course you *should* know how to do the job and if called upon ought not to hesitate in joining in, but no-one ever learns if the work is done for them. Once you have assigned the roles to your team, let them do their job. You may timetable 'check in' times but be sure to adapt them as you see the task getting done and your team's confidence in themselves growing. If they are faltering, find ways of empowering them to achieve rather than offering advice. If your team suggest ideas for improving current methods, then think about putting them into practice and be sure to acknowledge their success later if they work out. Even if the ideas have no real impact, this goes a long way to developing the individual strengths of your team members and will help create loyalty.

With an empowered team, you can turn your attention to developing yourself and your role.

Business brief

An article in *Forbes Magazine* states that 'managers must be leaders' (Morgan, 2015). This is because you need to establish trust within your team and inspire them to achieve, *and* you have a responsibility to drive your organisation forward. As a manager you are in a position to affect the organisational vision and contribute to growth. However, the only way you have the freedom to do so is if the rest of your department is functioning efficiently. Therefore it is essential that your team are able to do their tasks with confidence.

Your perspective must focus on the 'bigger picture', and part of that means seizing opportunities for growth. In a changing business world where the mantra is no longer 'the more loyal you are, the greater the reward' but rather 'the more essential your skills, the more you can demand' (call it the 'Footballer model' if you will[1]), you owe it to yourself, and your team to proactively develop personally and professionally.

Try this

1. Once your team is able to do their tasks, be available but do not micro-manage. Remember your job is to 'get things done', not 'do them' (see section 1.1).

2. Do not be afraid to learn from your team. Recognise talent and reward it where possible with remunerated responsibility. Remember that if you suppress your team's skills, you and your department will only ever be as good as your own skills.

3. Familiarise yourself with the plans for organisational growth and identify the skills that will be necessary to effect it.

4. Train yourself and your team as part of your commitment to CPD.

---

[1] Footballers come at a high price, but we're often willing to pay for those skills (The Secret Footballer, 2014).

5. Take a keen interest in the changing macro-environment. Conduct a SWOT (Strengths, Weaknesses, Opportunities, Threats) analysis on an annual basis to remain abreast of potential change.

6. Show corporate social responsibility by communicating changes in vision, mission or direction to your team so that they may also take an active part in their career direction.

REMEMBER

 Task first

 Empower staff through development and training

 Acknowledge success whether through financial or other means

 Monitor and respond to change

As entrepreneur Richard Branson states, on the Virgin website, 'Train people well enough so they can leave, treat them well enough so they don't want to.'

Reflection

- How did it work?

- What will I do next time?

References

Branson, R. (2014) Look after your staff. http://www.virgin.com/ richard-branson/look-after-your-staff.

Ogilvy, D. (2012) *The Unpublished David Ogilvy.* London: Profile Books.

Morgan, J. (2015) Why all managers must be leaders, *Forbes,* 21 January, http://www.forbes.com/sites/ jacobmorgan/2015/01/21/why-all-managers-must-be-leaders/ (retrieved July 2015).

The Secret Footballer (2014) *The Secret Footballer's Guide to the Modern Game.* Croydon: CPI Group (UK) Ltd.

Chapter **3**

Developing staff

3.1 Best invest in your staff

Before they start work you have made an investment in your staff, and this investment will either be returned or lost depending on how well you have recruited, retained and nurtured performance. Clever recruitment is essential not just to fill your skills gap, but in order to find someone who fits the organisational culture and vision – because you want them to stay. For high-flying staff, the recruitment process alone makes an impression, as does the ease with which a new employee settles in (and the respect with which an old employee goes) as it speaks volumes about the organisation itself. These are important, yet often overlooked factors that contribute to the new staff member's view of the organisation, and can affect performance.

Do this

Remember that an employee is an investment. Ask yourself how much research you'd do when buying a new phone. Make a note to do at least that much when recruiting a new member of staff.

3.2 Coaching as a management tool

Derived from the original transportation term 'coach', personal coaching is the act of bringing someone from one place to another, helping them to 'move forward or to create change' (Starr, 2011). Coaching happens through a 'structured conversation' – the structure of which is decided on and shaped by the coach – which equips the coachee with the time and space to focus on their circumstances, explore the issues they may be experiencing and generate their own solutions. The outcome of the coaching conversation usually includes improving in some way the coachee's own ability to think, learn and act, and empowering them to make better choices when faced with a similar situation in future. As such coaching is a form of empowerment.

However, many managers do not know how to do it. They prefer to give direct answers when advice is sought rather than using structured questioning to enable their staff member to come to a solution themselves. In situations where there is no time for discussion, coaching is of course not appropriate, but if managers become familiar with using coaching questions as a matter of course staff will seek less direct advice as they will be empowered and skilled to answer many of their own questions.

Coaching also demonstrates that you value what your team have to say because you have asked them what they think is appropriate to do. You have recognised their ability to answer the question they pose.

Coaching is the use of structured questioning and often follows a model. The 'Big picture' section will give you examples of questions that you can use when coaching your staff.

Do this

Ask yourself what you would do if a team member asked for your help. If the answer is 'Tell them what to do' or 'Let them figure it out for themselves', then go straight to section 3.2 and practise the coaching questions!

3.3 Making appraisals work

The appraisal originated as a form of organisational control. It was a means to justify labour costs and cuts, and therefore not unheard of for the next step to be a promotion or being released. However, the management of labour, and labour itself, is now more complex. It is, perhaps sadly, no longer the case that a high level of specialism in one area is required. More important nowadays is to have transferable skills that can be adapted to changes that occur within the job itself. With jobs being increasingly client centred, personal skills in most roles are as important as practical ones. Therefore, apart from in very specific circumstances, it is better to hire employees with rounded potential and develop it than look for someone who is highly skilled in one area with no room to improve.

As such, appraisals, when managed well (that is, correctly prepared for and conducted – see section 2.6), are an invaluable

learning tool and an opportunity to praise as well as to discuss concerns. The appraisal should be seen not as a means to an end but rather as a way to monitor continued progress. However, this is something that many managers must first realise themselves.

Do this

Check your appraisal pro forma. Is there a segment for praise? If not, add one, and see if you can get it added as standard.

3.4 Making the TNA meaningful

There is an abundance of paperwork in business. This is often because there is a need for everything to be evidenced and we cannot be relied on to do so without a pro forma. Unfortunately, forms are often completed as a matter of course, not because they are particularly useful documents. To demonstrate investment in staff development, most organisations require a TNA where the staff member identifies the skills they possess and those which they would like to develop. However, the paperwork alone is not sufficient. The TNA must be used for appraisals and CPD rather than sit in an employee's file as something checked off the list. 'Demonstrate' means 'show the existence or proof of', not just pay lip service to it with a few pieces of paperwork.

Do this
Have you seen your team's TNA? Find it, update it and use it by praising the skills they demonstrate and identifying ways to develop those they wish to enhance.

3.5 Training your team

Training must align with organisational strategy, and give the individual the opportunity to develop in a meaningful manner. Further, all training must demonstrate a return on investment whether that is in performance, financial turnover or retention. This raises the question of whether staff are better trained in house or by external companies. The former allows for training outcomes to match organisational goals precisely, but an external organisation can tailor training and often offer something extra which will serve your teams well in their own professional development. Remember also, that investment in-house can be very high if your training team is not always delivering training.

With so many courses on offer, managers sometimes forget that training needs to be relevant and have demonstrable results within the working arena. It also needs to be something that your team can implement right away or else the skills learned will be forgotten. Training should also be planned for and factored into the working day in order to ensure your department can function with fewer staff for the duration.

Do this

Identify which of your team have been on a training course recently. Ask them at their next briefing what they have learned and how they are using it.

3.6 The benefits of secondments

Not everyone will work in the same way. Secondments are a way of learning from other departments. Staff members can return with the knowledge they have acquired while on secondment, and can use this knowledge to improve practices within your department. Alternatively they may also return having used some of your procedures during their placement and reaffirming that your department works best (go you!). The opportunity to experience different organisational cultures and job roles assists professional growth and they may find their secondment offers them something which would be so beneficial to their personal career path that they cannot pass it up. When looking at the big picture, if someone in your team eventually moves floors, at least they are remaining with the organisation if not with your department.

Do this

Find out what opportunities exist for secondment in your organisation and let your team know.

3.7 Ask, don't assume (2)

Too often problems go unresolved because of a vicious cycle of assumptions on both sides:

1. The team assume the manager is too busy or too incompetent to make a change so they say nothing.

2. The manager assumes nothing is wrong because nothing has been said.

3. If something is said, often no solutions are offered. This might be because the team cannot think of one, do not think their solution will be acknowledged, or think that the manager will take the idea and the credit.

4. But with no solutions, the manager in this instance may assume the team have no ideas and will therefore implement their own idea which, from their own point of view, is a good solution . . . from the team's point of view, however, it may not be.

5. The team assumes the manager is incompetent.

(Go back to 1)

Do this

Ask your team to propose solutions to issues that they raise. They are the ones who know best what will work. If their solutions cannot be implemented, explain why. Clear lines of communication with your team are essential because assumption not only causes confusion, but can result in silos or silence.

3.1 Best invest in your staff

> 'Recently I was asked if I was going to fire an employee who made a mistake that cost the company $600,000. No, I replied, I just spent $600,000 training him. Why would I want somebody to hire his experience?'
>
> (Thomas John Watson Snr, cited in DeNisi and Griffin, 2015)

Why

Avoid continuous turnover. This affects productivity, and is demotivating and time-consuming. The more hours spent interviewing and inducting, the fewer spent doing your job. For your team, constantly seeing people come and go is demoralising, and may make them question if they should stay.

Focus on retention. Successful retention will depend on the individual needs of the staff member, the organisational

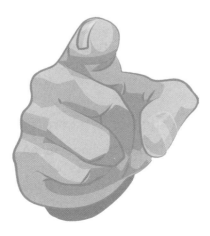

requirements (and rewards) and how closely they align, as well as on professional development and interpersonal treatment. It will also be affected by how your team perceive your treatment of them and their colleagues, with strong members of the team being more at risk of moving on than others. Performance is affected by both recruitment and retention behaviours.

Utilise the induction. Once you have recruited a new member of staff, the induction is not only necessary to get them up and running as fast as possible, but is also a way to make them feel welcome and to integrate them with the team. From then onwards, keep supporting them and maintain an awareness of their needs, not just for their benefit but also for that of your current team.

Business brief

The average cost of recruitment is around £30k (HR Review, 2014), which includes the cost of 'lost output' (when an employee leaves) and 'recruitment and absorption' (of the new worker). It then takes about six months before the new employee is performing at optimum capacity. You must work to retain them at least to this stage, and, if they are a good worker, beyond.

Whether one of your assets remains within your team depends on their personal motivations and their alignment with those of the organisation. It also depends on you. It is an old but common adage that 'people don't leave their jobs; they leave their managers'. This may be for a variety of reasons – a lack of faith in the manager's leadership ability; a personality clash; a perceived breach of a psychological contract; or even because of observed treatment of others in the team.

Business 'extra' - the 'honeymoon' (probation) period

The truth about 'probation' or 'honeymoon' periods. These are often built into employment contracts but have little legal standing, therefore it is questionable whether employers gain anything by having them. Where an employer (and arguably the employee) may benefit is in the period of notice that needs to be given to terminate employment during the probation period, which is often shorter than that required during within 'normal' employment.

There may also be an organisational procedure for dismissal during the probation period. However, your length of service which determines eligibility for statutory employment rights begins at the start of your employment (whether called 'probationary period' or not on your contract or not), as does your accrual of holiday and sickness time.

'Unfair dismissal' cannot be claimed unless the employee has worked in the organisation for two years. If, for example, an employee wishes to bring a case of 'Unfair dismissal on the grounds of discrimination' they will be allowed to bring it under a case of 'Discrimination'.

For more exemptions, please visit the "Compact Law Website: www.compactlaw.co.uk/free-legal-information/employment-law/ exceptions-for-unfair-dismissal.html

Try this

1. Know what you are looking for from the outset. If the job description needs to be changed with a view to finding someone who is a better match for the organisation's goals, take this opportunity to change it.

2. Book the venue and recruitment personnel and ensure everyone knows how to use the recruitment pro formas if scoring candidates.

3. Take the recruitment process seriously. You should consider not only whether the candidate has the right skills but also if their personality will make them a good fit for the team.

4. Consider an assessment day, of which the interview is one part. This offers a better indication of each candidate's overall performance level.

5. Remember to let your interviewees speak. Managers often end up answering their own questions and then come away thinking the interview went better than it did.

6. Never forget that recruitment is auditable – DO NOT write 'funny' acronyms, e.g. NL (nice legs) on the score sheet.

7. Do not make promises you cannot or do not have the authority to keep.

8. Make sure you treat your exiting staff well as this speaks volumes about how you will treat your new ones!

9. Ensure you have a means to progress, develop and reward your staff.

Reflection

- How did it work?

```
┌─────────────────────────────────────────────────┐
│                                                 │
│                                                 │
│                                                 │
│                                                 │
│                                                 │
└─────────────────────────────────────────────────┘
```

- What will I do next time?

```
┌─────────────────────────────────────────────────┐
│                                                 │
│                                                 │
│                                                 │
│                                                 │
│                                                 │
└─────────────────────────────────────────────────┘
```

References

DeNisi, A. and Griffin, R. (2015) *HR3: Human Resources.* Andover: Cengage Learning.

HR Review (2014) It costs over 30k to replace a staff member, *HR Review,* 25 February, http://www.hrreview.co.uk/hr-news/recruitment/it-costs-over-30k-to-replace-a-staff-member/50677 (retrieved July 2015).

3.2 Coaching as a management tool

> *'Coaching makes things better in the workplace. It develops a human organisation and improves individual and organisational durability.'*
>
> (Ruth Metz, 2011)

Why

More than any form of advice, coaching *empowers* your staff. You are asking them for their opinion in a safe context and you get to hear what they have to say. If their response indicates a training need you can correct them at that point and ensure they get help as required. More often than not, however, their ideas will be valuable and different from your own; coaching thus affords you the opportunity to learn.

Coaching can support personal development, and thus aid the retention, recruitment and performance of positive, motivated staff. It is both a way of supporting staff and a style of management.

Business brief

As an industry, coaching is continuing to grow – a 2009 survey from the Chartered Institute of Personnel and Development (CIPD, 2009) found that 'coaching is the most effective talent management activity used by organizations', whilst a survey on behalf of the International Coach Federation (ICF, 2009) found that coaching improved self-confidence, communication, interpersonal skills, work performance and relationships (both cited in Starr, 2011).

Coaching falls within the second quadrant of Hersey's (1984) Situational Leadership Grid. This is where the use of the term in business causes confusion. Within the Situational Leadership Grid, the term is used with reference to sports coaching. Coaching in sport (where the term originally derived) is more directive than within business or personal development. However, the sense in which it is used in this chapter, and how the author advocates its use in the workplace derives more from 'life coaching' – that is, coaching as its evolved definition.

The coach (or the coaching manager) uses a series of questions to help the coachee (or team member) explore their own thoughts and ideas on the situation at hand. Through this the coachee/team member is able to generate their own solutions. This is essential because it means they are also more likely to action them.

If coaching becomes embedded as a style of management, you will have created a culture of coaching which will, in turn, encourage your staff to coach junior team members. All of this at no extra training cost.

Try this

Coaching is best implemented in two ways.

1. Executive coaching – external coaching
   - Referral from line manager/self-referral (line manager aware).
   - Or private clients.
   - A series of four to six sessions is arranged over a period of three to six months.*
   - In a referral case a review with the line manager should take place after the third and the sixth session; with private clients the review process will be between coach and coachee, and the line manager will not be involved.

*NB: Coaching needs to have a finite duration as it means that work problems are swiftly addressed and sessions are always meaningful.

2. Management training – in-house coaches
   - Training leaders and managers via an ICF-recognised course.
   - Leaders and managers implement a coaching culture and this results in their teams coaching others as a matter of course.

(NHS North West Leadership Academy, 2015)

Practice using the following coaching models (note that there are many; these are the two the author uses):

- CIGAR

The acronym CIGAR stands for Current reality, the Ideal position, the Gaps (between the current and ideal), the Action available to take, and Review - a reflection on the action taken.

- GROW

The acronym GROW stands for Goal, the current Reality, the Options you can take and the Will you have to follow those options through.

Each of the headings describes the sort of questions you need to ask when discussing the issue at hand. Once you have explored the first area to your satisfaction, you move on to the next.

Using the GROW model for example:

Example questions you might ask

G	Goal	• What would you like the situation to look like?
R	Reality	• How would you describe the situation? • How might X describe the situation?
O	Options	• What would help close the gap? • Who have you asked for help?
W	Will	• Who **can** you ask for help? • On a scale of 1–10 how likely are you to follow that course of action?

For more information on the GROW model, please see *Coaching for Performance* by John Whitmore (2009, Nicholas Brealey Publishing)

Tips

- For every scale answer that is 7 or below, always ask 'What would make it an 8?'.
- For every 'I don't know' respond with 'Imagine if you did.'
- The reason for this is that people have often practised socially desirable answers and these responses indicate a thought that has not yet wholly formed and is therefore closer to their actual thinking, the exploration of which helps them better move forward.
- Be aware that coaching needs time, and is therefore not appropriate for every occasion.

Reflection

- How did it work?

- What will I do next time?

References

CIPD (2009) Taking the temperature of coaching, summer 2009 hot topic, www.cipd.co.uk/NR/rdonlyres/E27F313C-FFBC-466F-84D8-A240893A2A22/0/Taking_temperature_coaching.pdf (retrieved July 2015).

Hersey, P. (1984) *The Situational Leader: The Other 59 Minutes*. New York, NY: Warner Books.

ICF (2009) ICF Global Coaching Client Study, http://coachfederation.org/about/landing.cfm?ItemNumber=830 (retrieved July 2015).

Metz, R.F. (2011) *Coaching in the Library: A Management Strategy for Achieving Excellence*. Chicago, IL: American Library Association.

NHS Leadership Academy (2014), Embedding a Coaching Culture in the NHS, www.nwacademy.nhs.uk/sites/default/files/leader-june-2015.pdf (retrieved Jan 2016).

Starr, J. (2011) *The Coaching Manual*. Harlow: Pearson Education.

3.3 Making appraisals work

'What interested me was not news, but appraisal. What I sought was to grasp the flavour of a man, his texture, his impact, what he stood for, what he believed in, what made him what he was and what colour he gave to the fabric of his time.'

(John Gunther, cited in Zoellner, 2007)

Why

An appraisal is an(other) opportunity for you to speak directly with your team. You are able to learn more about their professional goals, and in your mind see if they align well with the organisation's. This is not a covert process; it is an opportunity to discuss openly how your staff wish to progress and, realistically, if your organisation can support them. Use the appraisal to raise any concerns, and of course to praise – both with evidence.

Your staff must understand that appraisals are not necessarily 'the truth', but a discussion of how the people interviewed perceive them. The opportunity to see themselves through the eyes of others can be extremely thought-provoking and powerful, and with this knowledge you can invite them to change the perception – or accept it.

Many organisations have an appraisals pro forma – prepare for the appraisal, and ensure that your team prepare too. If you value it, so will they.

Business brief

With less time to meet face to face, the appraisal can be a welcome opportunity to re-engage with discussion, re-affirm relationships, as well as re-align goals and professional direction in person.

An appraisal is an organisational form of the 'Johari Window' (Luft and Ingham, 1955) – a discussion of what is known to yourself, to others, or to both, and can often reveal the 'blind' area, giving you (or those you are appraising) the opportunity to reflect on the insights it provides.

The appraisal also forms an important piece of evidence to demonstrate that your team are being given the support they need so that they are not disadvantaged due to age, disability or any other factor. An issue raised within an appraisal must be recorded and dealt with.

Try this

Make sure YOU measure up as an appraiser!

1. Plan for each appraisal – be very clear on the message you want your staff to leave with.

2. Complete any appraisal pro formas and have evidence to support all points. (Evidence can come from client feedback, observation, colleague reports and so on.)

3. Allow your staff to prepare – make sure they know the time and date of the appraisal at least a week in advance and try not to reschedule it unless you absolutely have to.

4. Should you have to cancel or postpone apologise to the member of staff – they are likely to be nervous, and you can expect them to have prepared.

5. Set aside a time to conduct the appraisal with no interruptions, and in a private room. (Note – it does not have to be your room as this can be intimidating. Remember appraisals are a discussion as much as a review.)

6. If you have to raise an issue, present the facts alone and ask your member of staff to relate their version of events.

7. During the appraisal listen to your staff. Explore issues with them using the coaching techniques in section 3.2.

8. Focus on the future, but do not give short shrift to the past as this may make your staff feel undervalued, especially if they have something they wish to discuss.

9. Agree an action plan with SMART goals. Try to have no more than three as more can be unmanageable.

10. Agree a review time and date.

11. You might even ask your team what else they feel would make appraisals more productive – if you have conducted them well, your team will now perceive them positively and may be more willing to contribute to making them a development tool.

12. If you need support in your own personal communication skills (e.g. making eye contact, sincerity, clarity of voice), seek it out prior to the appraisal.

Reflection

- How did it work?

- What will I do next time?

```


```

References

Luft, J. and Ingham, H. (1955) The Johari Window, a graphic model of interpersonal awareness, in *Proceedings of the Western Training Laboratory in Group Development*. Los Angeles, CA: University of California.

Zoellner, T. (2007) *Homemade Biography: How to Collect, Record, and Tell the Life Story of Someone You Love*. New York, NY: Griffin.

3.4 Making the TNA meaningful

'Knowing is not enough; we must apply. Willing is not enough; we must do.'

(Johann Wolfgang von Goethe)

Why

The TNA may be part of the induction or the appraisal process and is often seen as 'another exercise in form filling'. As such, on completion it is often filed never to be seen again, or added to a spreadsheet of sorts to ensure that the member of staff who has completed it is up to date with any mandatory training. It often serves little other purpose, but that does not prevent it being a long document that takes time to complete for both manager and staff member. As with appraisals, it is essential to make the TNA meaningful. With most paperwork, if it has to be done it will take part of your day that could be spent doing 'actual' work, therefore it needs to be useful and much more than a box-ticking exercise.

Business brief

Mike Cooley (1982) in his book *Architect or Bee?* proposed that while computers were originally introduced to the design world to give architects more freedom to create (like the bee), the outcome unfortunately resulted in the 'freed' mind space being taken up with processes as the architect first had to learn new systems to use the computer. Once those processes were learned, however, technology assisted in enhancing design beyond imagination. The TNA to the manager is like the first computer to the architect. It is extra work.

However, if the TNA can be utilised as a working curriculum vitae of skills, or as a development plan, it becomes a document that can be referred to and updated as new qualifications are gained and later safe time when your team (or department) wishes to progress.

It is an achievement list for each appraisal and a written reminder of personal, professional and departmental progress and can

assist with the inevitable 'update of the CV' as members of your team prepare for promotion or to move on (or both).

Try this

1. Make sure your organisation's TNA doesn't just list the skills that employees should have in the form of tick boxes. Allow the staff member space to comment on their abilities.

2. Ensure that there is a means to request further training in certain areas.

3. Read the TNA and use it when requesting staff training.

4. Retain the TNA and use it as part of the appraisal process, i.e. update it as an objective and ongoing measure of progress.

Reflection

- How did it work?

- What will I do next time?

References

Cooley, M. (1982) *Architect or Bee? The Human/technology Relationship.* Boston, MA: South End Press.

Goethe, J.W. (n.d.) quoted in Purnell, L.D. (2012) *Transcultural Health Care: A Culturally Competent Approach.* Philadelphia, PA: FA Davis Publishing.

3.5 Training your team

> *'Excellence is an art won by training and habituation. We do not act rightly because we have virtue or excellence, but we rather have those because we have acted rightly. We are what we repeatedly do. Excellence, then, is not an act but a habit.'*
>
> (Aristotle)

Why

Training is often viewed as the 'poor relative' within an organisation. Staff grimace at having to undertake mandatory training courses, and managers begrudgingly view it as a necessary evil for completing their employee tick boxes. With moves towards e-learning and in-house staff often delivering training courses in addition to carrying out their 'real' job, it is no wonder that its value is being overlooked. When the trainer may lack the necessary skills, *and* the quality of the session is questionable, a self-fulfilling prophecy that 'training is a waste of time' ensues.

Business brief

Vanthournout et al. (2006) charted the return on investment Accenture received once they had committed to a focus on training as a means to retain staff and increase performance. Instead of slashing the training budget in an effort to cut costs, Accenture instead invested in it, finding that their staff appreciated the interest, stayed longer, encouraged people to join the organisation and put what they learned into practice. In addition, their in-house learning and development team could be outsourced to apply

their skills elsewhere and so bring financial benefit to Accenture. 'For every dollar Accenture invests in learning, the organisation receives that dollar back plus an additional $3.25 in measurable value to its bottom line – in other words, a 353% return on learning' (Vanthournout et al., 2006).

If the organisational goals are supported, and what is learned is put into practice, the life of the training is prolonged. Training, if done well, can be one of your organisation's most financially viable and valuable resources, as what is learned is ploughed straight back into organisational performance – and good in-house training can even be outsourced.

Try this

1. Use the TNA and appraisal development pages to source training that is meaningful to your staff.

2. If you do not have an in-house department, ask Procurement to see which providers the organisation has a pre-existing relationship with. (This can help financially.)

3. Ensure that your training requests match organisational development goals.

4. Ask staff to report back on what they learned from the training sessions.

5. Ensure that what is learned can be put into practice within the department.

6. Use an evaluation model such as Kirkpatrick and Kirkpatrick's (1994) structure to assess and review the return on investment. The model covers:

  (a) The **reaction** to the session. This is ascertained through the sheets given at the end of the session ... known somewhat disparagingly as 'happy sheets' as many learning and development departments feel that participants are likely just to rate everything 'good' if they had fun.

  (b) The **learning** that has taken place. This may be measured through summative assessment.

  (c) Post-training **behaviour**. This is commonly obtained through a follow-up session with the trainee's line manager three to six months after the programme, where observations of the changes that have occurred are discussed.

  (d) **Results or return** on learning. This is the fundamental success of training and can be measured in retention or performance figures.

7. Make time for your own training.

Reflection

- How did it work?

- What will I do next time?

```

```

References

Aristotle (1999) *Nicomachean Ethics,* trans. Irwin, T.H. Indianapolis, IN: Hackett Publishing Company.

Kirkpatrick, D.L. and Kirkpatrick, J.D. (1994) *Evaluating Training Programs.* San Francisco, CA: Berrett-Koehler Publishers.

Vanthournout, D., Olson, K., Ceisel, J., White, A., Waddington, T., Barfield, T., Desai, S. and Mindrum, C. (2006) *Return on Learning – Training for High Performance at Accenture.* Chicago, IL: Agate.

3.6 The benefits of secondments

'A change is as good as a rest.'

(Proverb)

Why

Your team can be your learning channel and secondments are a good way to become familiar with other departments, learn different ways of working and sometimes appreciate that you are doing a good job. One opportunity that secondments afford is the chance to understand the organisation in a more holistic manner. How does one department affect another? How do our actions impact on others? That alone can assist more collaborative working. Another opportunity is for your staff to experience different management cultures. Large organisations in particular may have departments that are quite disparate in nature; however, it can mean that certain departmental cultures

may be more suited to certain personalities than others. As such, if there has been a personality clash within your department a secondment can afford the necessary space, may result in a better fit and might ultimately mean that a good member of staff is not lost to the organisation as a whole.

Business brief

Reasons for secondments have been divided by McKenzie (2003) into five key areas: (i) secondments can be developmental and thus mutually beneficial to the secondee and the two departments (the one left and the one entered); (ii) secondments might be strategic, for example when a department needs a particular skill and someone is brought in to fulfil that need temporarily; (iii) they may be an alternative to a tribunal; (iv) they may be an attempt to keep a valued worker within an organisation; or (v) they may be a form of transition to support with redundancy. Whatever the reason, the development of skills is a large part.

Bond (2002) and Critchley (2002) identified nine benefits of secondments on the nursing profession: security, enablement, career enhancement, opportunity, networking, diversity, motivation education and nurture.

View secondments as an excellent opportunity to progress the skills set of your staff, as well as retain their loyalty.

Try this

If a member of staff is considering a secondment be very clear about the following:

1. Where they will be working and any new regulations they may need to meet.

2. How long the secondment is to be for.

3. What skills they will learn/offer.

4. Who will replace them in your department.

5. Whether the secondment can be terminated early in the event of any issues.

6. What those potential issues may be.

7. Whether they need extra training or insurance and whether this affects their pay, holiday entitlement and other statutory benefits.

8. Who will deal with supervision/appraisals/disciplinary issues.

9. How they will be re-integrated back into the original department.

10. How the organisation will learn from the shared experience.

Reflection

- How did it work?

- What will I do next time?

```
```

References

Bond, P. (2002) Changing places, *Nursing Management UK,* 9(8), 12–16.

Cambridge Dictionaries Online (2015) http://dictionary.cambridge.org/dictionary/english/a-change-is-as-good-as-a-rest (retrieved August 2015).

Critchley, D. (2002) Second sight, *Nursing Management UK,* 9(7), 12–13.

McKenzie, J. (2003) *Secondment Benefits,* McKenzie and Associates website, www.secondments.com (retrieved July 2015).

3.7 Ask, don't assume (2)

'Don't make assumptions. Find the courage to ask questions and to express what you really want. Communicate with others as clearly as you can to avoid misunderstandings. With just this one agreement, you can completely transform your life.'

(Don Miguel Ruiz, 2015)

Why

People change and it can be a long time between appraisals to find out why a previously motivated worker now seems to be disheartened, or a heretofore quiet worker is suddenly becoming more active, if you do not ask. Often when you choose to assume it is because you don't want to know the answer, and yet communicating openly may reveal the reality to be less problematic than what you have been assuming and enable a shared solution to be generated. Or it may simply be arrogance that is making you assume – in which case you are more than likely to be wrong!

Business brief

In any conversation it is important to realise that there are four levels of listening (Starr, 2011). These may be described as follows:

Cosmetic – where the listener is not really engaged, but nonetheless makes the right sort of noises: 'uh-huh', 'mm' and so on.

Conversational – where there is a level of engagement in the conversation.

Active – where the listener asks questions and probes further. They may also paraphrase and summarise statements back to the speaker.

Deep – This is the level of listening that goes beyond what is actually being said. It can include noticing body language, or repetitive phrases, or changes in tone which can all prompt the listener to enquire further into a particular area.

(Starr, 2011)

The more you are able to engage deep listening the more you will learn about your team. Even something that you think you know about a team member can be challenged when addressed directly as body language can betray the words spoken. Even if you are worried about the answer, it is always best to ask the question and then listen – with your ears and eyes.

Try this

1. Practise deep listening – outside the workplace as well as within. Like any skill, it can only be developed with use.

2. Take opportunities to talk with your staff, even if it is only small talk. This can go some way to establishing rapport and building trust so that when you need to talk about something significant it is not a daunting prospect. (However, avoid over-familiarity as it is important to retain your professionalism.)

3. If the situation arises where a serious or difficult conversation needs to take place, consider having it in a neutral location rather than your office as it offsets the perception of power.

Reflection

- How did it work?

- What will I do next time?

References

Ruiz, D.M. (2015) *The Four Agreements, A Toltec Wisdom Book,* ExpressionsofSpirit.com, http://www.expressionsofspirit.com/4-agreements.htm (retrieved August 2015).

Starr, J. (2011) *The Coaching Manual.* Harlow: Pearson.

Chapter 4

Motivating staff

4.1 Be aware that not everyone will care as much as you

As a manager, you are closer to the organisational values and vision than your team. People are motivated to work for different reasons. Some work to live and they will be extrinsically motivated – mainly by money or time off. Others may have a greater intrinsic drive, especially if they are in an organisation with in which they hope to progress. By moving into a management role, you too have an intrinsic drive, but just remember not all of your team will. Motivation is about having a variety of methods to encourage and inspire, and if you can get your team engaged on a project-by-project basis (even if they are not engaged with the organisation as a whole), that's a bonus.

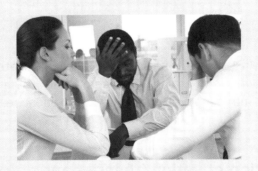

Do this
Make a list of all the things that have motivated you in the past – do one of them for your team tomorrow!

4.2 Extrinsic motivation (theories and practice)

Incentives such as pay, time off in lieu (TOIL), or other benefits may motivate your team to perform efficiently and effectively, but should those incentives be stopped or changed, a rapid decline in productivity often follows. While extrinsic motivating factors are effective for new staff or those who 'work to live', they are less successful in inciting those who have a passion for their vocation or have chosen the organisation within which they wish to progress. They are also sometimes out of your direct control and therefore could become a false promise. A mixture of extrinsic and intrinsic motivation is required at all times – not just when you want something done!

Do this

Ask yourself – and be honest – do you only motivate your staff when you want something? Choose another thing off the list you've just made (above), and do it . . . just because.

4.3 Intrinsic motivation (theories and practice)

Intrinsic motivation can be as simple as praise, recognition and acknowledgement. Opportunities to develop as well as the offer of support or the knowledge that help is there should your staff need it can be very motivating. Intrinsic motivation penetrates the core of why someone wants to work, and is what drives them when all other circumstances seem less than positive. However, it is most often overlooked and once it wanes, your best staff leave.

Do this

Ask your staff to write down on Post-its what they love about their jobs . . . get them to stick them up on the office door or noticeboard.

4.4 What do you believe about your team?

Actors and sports stars are only as good as their last performance. Unfortunately humans have a tendency to 'compartmentalise' and you may find you are labelling a team member unfairly just because of something they said or did – which you may even have perceived incorrectly. If this affects your behaviour towards them (positively or negatively) it can affect your relationship with them,

and may even sometimes impact on your relationship with the rest of your team. You might be labouring under a misapprehension – look at your beliefs and assumptions and test them every so often!

Do this

Write down one assumption you have about your team members, then look for evidence to support or refute it. Challenge your own thinking.

4.5 The truth behind team building

You don't need to go white-water rafting or change tyres on F1 cars to ensure you have a motivated team. It's not so much the task as the day-to-day (emotional) investment you have in your team that counts! 'Team days' can sometimes be viewed with suspicion – as if 'that's the manager paying lip service to team building'. This is especially so in a team that is already dysfunctional. However, behaviour is dynamic, and although it can take time, attitudes can change . . . but not as the result of one day, no matter how thrilling. Building a team relationship is the same as any relationship – it's the little, seemingly insignificant things that count, and these mount up. It is also those very things that can tip the balance if your staff consider leaving for another job.

Do this

Reflect on 'team days' you have enjoyed. Identify what made them special. Use *that* as your guide when planning the next one.

4.6 Emotional labour

Motivating a team also requires emotional support for the manager – be mindful of your own support needs and network. Interpersonal relationships are important in successful team management, but they can be one-sided. You may feel that you are giving support, advice and motivation and getting little in return. What you are most likely receiving is productivity and success in your department because your team is feeling positive – and that is as it should be. Your team, however, are not there to make you feel loved. If you think of emotion as water, and yourself as a sponge, having to contain the anxieties of your team, of course means you too need emotional support . . . a sort of metaphorical hug. That, however, must come from personal resilience, colleagues or your own line management, not your team or the interpersonal balance can be detrimentally shifted.

Do this

Identify who you turn to when you need support. If the list is empty, fill it with at least one name . . . it can even be someone from a social media network such as LinkedIn.

4.7 Making meetings motivational

Meetings are a great opportunity to brief, troubleshoot and motivate, but all too often they are considered by all to be a waste of time. Yet, if a meeting is clearly organised (time, date, venue, agenda) with a workable format and a strong chair, it can be one of the most positive parts of a day.

Do this

Look at your last meeting agenda. Does it allocate an amount of time to discuss each point? If so, did you stick to these? When you put together the agenda for your next meeting, assign realistic times to each point and be strict about moving through the list – if necessary, arrange a time for after the meeting to expand on matters that need to be discussed with the relevant people.

4.1 Be aware that not everyone will care as much as you

'Anger, resentment and jealousy doesn't change the heart of others – it only changes yours.'

(Sharon L. Alder, 2011)

Why

If you remain aware of the fact that not everyone cares as much as you then you are better placed to look for creative forms of motivation rather than being upset that your initial attempts are having little effect. (Negativity consumes a lot of brain power and creativity and is therefore unproductive.) Motivation, as with all behaviours, is dynamic and therefore what may motivate someone at one time may not at another. It is best to try to encourage your team to engage with the project or task they are doing as completion will be its own reward, but this is not always possible. Also, never forget that just because *you* think a task is exciting, that doesn't mean the person doing it will agree!

Business brief

Theories of motivation range from being money orientated, e.g. Taylor (1911) or McGregor's Theory X ([1966] 2006), to more personal incentives, e.g. having social needs met (Mayo [1933] 2003), self-actualisation (being the best you can be) (Maslow, 1967), or McGregor's Theory Y ([1966] 2006), and the creative manager uses a mixture of them all. A bonus (especially if it is not perceived as significant) will not motivate a disheartened worker in the same way as praise and acknowledgement might, and a team member who needs the money won't necessarily care if the task you give them is meaningful as long as it enables them to work the extra hours. However, if you can convince them of the importance of their role within the wider organisation, you will find that motivation becomes less important than recognition and acknowledgement of performance.

Try this

1. Find out what incentives you are able to offer (e.g. time off in lieu, flexi hours, bonuses, cake or treat funds).
2. Find out what drives your team and try to motivate them accordingly.
3. Ask colleagues about their approaches to motivation – what works, what doesn't.
4. Ensure that you know the significance of all your team members within the wider organisation – and tell them!

5. Praise and acknowledge good work. Be present within your team so you know when to reward them.

Reflection

- How did it work?

- What will I do next time?

References

Alder, S.L. (2011) *300 Questions to Ask Your Parents Before it's too Late*. Springville, UT: Horizon.

Maslow, A.H. (1967) A theory of metamotivation: the biological rooting of the value-life, *Journal of Humanistic Psychology,* 7(2): 93–127.

Mayo, G.E. ([1933] 2003) *The Human Problems of an Industrial Civilization*. London: Routledge, reprint.

McGregor, D. ([1966] 2006) *The Human Side of Enterprise*. New York, NY: McGraw-Hill Professional, reprint.

Taylor, F.W. (1911) *The Principles of Scientific Management*. New York, NY and London: Harper & Brothers.

4.2 Extrinsic motivation (theories and practice)

'Motivation is everything. You can do the work of two people, but you can't be two people. Instead, you have to inspire the next guy down the line and get him to inspire his people.'

(Lee Iacocca)

Why

Extrinsic motivation is *any* motivation that comes from outside the individual. This can include money, time, promotion and also praise and recognition – even though the latter are more personal. Often extrinsic motivation is the dominant motivator for finding a job in the first instance, and these strategies are therefore the ones that you will often consider first.

Business brief

It is too easy to think that if someone is being paid to do something that is motivation enough. Praise and recognition are also motivators. They are the easiest to give, yet they are most often overlooked. In a study conducted among members of staff regarding their relationships with their manager, common responses were:

> 'No-one notices what I do until I'm not there – then they have a go that things aren't done.'
>
> 'When you do a good job, it doesn't matter, but if you make a mistake, they are on top of you for ages.'
>
> 'Once a manager even said to a team "You get so many cards and emails from people – they come to me, so you don't ever get them. But you're doing a good job." I know what he was trying to say – but WHY don't they ever get them? If he hadn't turned up for the last five minutes of their training session – and even then we had to force him there – they would never have known.'
>
> 'It was like she had just gone round everyone to make sure she said something, it was like "Thank you for showing up."'

(Tang, 2012)

Get praise right, and you'll be rewarded in performance.

Try this

1. Interpersonal motivations such as acknowledgement through comments, emails, cards or perhaps a 'cake Friday', whether from yourself, colleagues or clients, should always be shared.

2. Include a 'celebration' section in team meetings or briefings, making appreciation habitual.

3. As a general rule, make praise public but discipline private – however, you need to know your team. If some team members are easily embarrassed or are always receiving praise, tell them that is why you are praising them in private!

4. Any time you need to reiterate rules, remind your team *why* those rules are in place.

5. Find out your remit for offering financial and working time rewards, but use them sparingly.

6. Be present – know what is happening in your team and acknowledge the performance as well as any improvement. If you need to, keep your own record of who has been praised and look for ways to praise others who haven't had recognition for a while.

7. Be genuine in your praise. There is nothing worse than praise for praise's sake.

Reflection

- How did it work?

- What will I do next time?

References

Iacocca, L. (1986), *Iacocca: An Autobiography.* New York, NY: Bantam.
Tang, A. (2015) *Love's Labours Redressed, Reframing Emotional Labour.* Saarbrücken: LAP Lambert Academic Publishing.

4.3 Intrinsic motivation (theories and practice)

'You can motivate by fear and you can motivate by reward. But both these methods are only temporary. The only lasting thing is self-motivation.'

(Homer Rice, cited in Corbin et al., 2014)

Why

While people are drawn to organisations for extrinsic reasons (money, career development, recognition), their choice of

organisational field is often more intrinsic. Therefore they have often applied for a job which they not only feel they can do, but, to a great extent, *want* to do. This means that if the job is due to change, unless the change is desired or understood, motivation is easily affected.

Business brief

Menzies Lyth (1960) conducted a study on nurses working in a ward of terminally ill patients. In order to 'protect' them against the emotional pressures of the job, management implemented changes such as rotating nurses on a regular basis so that they were unable to form too great an attachment to their patients, and encouraged them to refer to patients not by their name but by their illness. This completely contradicted the very reasons why the nurses had entered the caring profession in the first place and had a negative effect on motivation and performance. While thinking they were acting in the best interests of their staff, the management had got it very wrong.

The study may have been carried out some decades ago, but the point remains valid: that, too often work-based decisions still get made by those who do not engage in the practice on a regular basis. Learn what the job means from those *doing* it – or do it yourself for a while!

For a great video on how to help staff stay intrinsically motivated, check out FISH! Philosophy at http://www.fishphilosophy.com/.

Try this

1. Rather than thinking you know best, speak to your team to try to generate solutions for problems (the 'Thinking Hats' technique at the end of this chapter may help). Be clear with restrictions, i.e. if you cannot do something, make that clear.

2. If a change needs to be made to the role of one of your team members, make sure your team understand why

this change is necessary in terms of the bigger picture. If a change negatively affects how someone does their job, they are better able to accept it if they understand it is for the 'greater good'.

3. Cutting costs is not usually accepted as part of the 'greater good' unless you can show it is the only way for everyone to retain their jobs.

4. If you are changing a job description, then make sure this is also done through HR. If it is possible to add an extrinsic incentive to soften the blow, this can sometimes help the period of adjustment.

5. Monitor changes to the job, and do not be too proud to change them again if they are clearly not working out (following steps 1–4 to do so).

Reflection

- How did it work?

- What will I do next time?

References

Corbin, C., McConnell, K., Le Masurier, G., Corbin, D.E. and Farrar, T.D. (2014) *Health Opportunities Through Physical Education with Web Resources.* Pudsey: Human Kinetics Publishers.

FISH! Philosophy (n.d.) http://www.fishphilosophy.com/ (retrieved August 2015).

Menzies Lyth, I. (1960) Social systems as a defence against anxiety, *Human Relations,* 13, 95–121.

4.4 What do you believe about your team?

'Begin challenging your own assumptions. Your assumptions are your windows on the world. Scrub them off every once in a while, or the light won't come in.'

(Alan Alda, 2006)

Why

Performance is dynamic, and you need to be working with what you see at the present time rather than on past experience. If you don't, then some of your team may feel unsupported, while others may receive favourable treatment for things they have not done. While it is most likely that a team member who has performed well in the past will continue to do so, if you work on assumption rather than what is happening you may miss when a good team member is struggling, or when someone suddenly finds a task very easy and excels at it.

Business brief

'The most successful people need your support and development too – they won't always ask ... don't let the reasons you hired them be the very reasons they leave' (Tang, 2015). Past performance can be a predictor of future behaviour, but it is a fallible one. It is better to be aware of *patterns* of performance and seek to test your perceptions through discussion with your team, or with others with whom they have worked. Note your own responses too. Do you always respond to someone who calls loudly – if so, are you neglecting others? Are the people staying below the parapet truly happy or are they looking for an escape route? Is your team's behaviour a reflection of your own? Remember that we are fundamentally egocentric and automatically only see things from one perspective, and to get a better idea of the full picture we need to look more widely. If you ignore the person who seems quiet, you may lose them to another organisation. If you are constantly trying to help the one who shouts the loudest, the chance to empower them gets smaller. If a high flier seems to be doing ok – just take the time to double check that this is the case.

Try this

1. Remain approachable and listen to your team when they choose to talk to you.

2. Remember that when someone (especially someone very capable) asks for help it is often because they have struggled silently for some time!

3. Be aware that high fliers can need help, and it is far more important to retain them rather than those who simply shout the loudest – whom you may never please anyway!

4. Remember that the reason why you don't delegate jobs that you wouldn't do yourself is partly because sometimes you may need at least the basic knowledge to teach others.

5. If you notice that someone is excelling at a task, acknowledge it and use the opportunity to update their TNA. Look for more opportunities to involve them in that area in future if they are enjoying it.

6. Remember that sometimes people fall into team roles not because they enjoy them, but out of habit.

7. Ultimately, remain aware!

Reflection

- How did it work?

- What will I do next time?

References

Alda, A. (2006) *Never Have Your Dog Stuffed and Other Things I've Learned.* New York, NY: Random House.

Tang, A. (2015) Blog post, High fliers need your helping hand too, https://www.linkedin.com/pulse/channel/leadership_and_management (retrieved August 2015).

4.5 The truth behind team building

> 'If you want to build a ship, don't drum up people together to collect wood and don't assign them work ... teach them to long for the endless immensity of the sea.'
>
> (Antoine de Saint-Exupery)

Why

Team building days, while often enjoyable at the time, and clearly sometimes an investment, do little more than energise staff temporarily. This certainly gives the impression that the working environment is positive and often means that any cracks are papered over for a while. However, in the long term, if a team is dysfunctional this needs to be addressed, and a team building day that focuses on 'having fun' alone is not going to do it, but may simply put off the inevitable breakdown a while longer. What you need to do is understand the foundation of a team – the common goal. Then get your team to respect each other and each other's skills, recognising that they need to work together to achieve what they want. The premise behind 'team building days' is simple – it is not about individual tasks and jobs, but everyone wanting that project to succeed.

Business brief

If a dysfunctional team falls within any of the five areas identified by Lencioni (2002) – see Chapter 2 – it is obvious that a 'fun day' is not going to address the problem. While Sherif et al.'s (1954) 'Robbers' Cave' experiment found that conflict can be broken down by forcing people to work together (on a task they can succeed in), seeing their behaviour, engaging in guided reflection on the reasons for this behaviour and how it is perceived, and discussing how they can move through the conflict is the only way to build a team.

Try this

1. Sometimes a 'listening event' – especially in a dysfunctional team – is of more help at first. However, the 'Thinking Hat' technique (section 4.7) could be used to avoid the event becoming a 'moan fest'.

2. An immersive learning option is to try one of the 'Exit Games' events that take place all over the country (see www. exitgames.co.uk). In these events, groups of two to ten people are put in a room together from which they have to escape within 60 minutes. The activity itself, with the stress involved in working under time pressure, is enough to reveal the different communication styles of the participants, but in addition, all participants are watched (and with permission can often be recorded) on video camera. At the time of writing A Great Escape in Bletchley, UK and Pfeffermind Games running 'Mission Accepted' in Berlin, Germany, currently offer the only CPD accredited 'Escape Package' where teams engage in the activity and then have the opportunity to watch and reflect on their performance through a guided debrief and training session.

3. Nevertheless, if you are running a team building day, remember that it is an investment. If you have been slipshod with the venue, the refreshments and the activities, it speaks volumes about how much you value your team!

Reflection

- How did it work?

- What will I do next time?

References

de Saint-Exupery, A. (n.d.) BrainyQuote.com, http://www.brainyquote.com/quotes/quotes/a/antoinedes121261.html (retrieved August 2015).

Lencioni, P.M. (2002) *The Five Dysfunctions of a Team: A Leadership Fable*. Chichester: John Wiley & Sons.

Sherif, M. (1954) Experimental study of positive and negative inter-group attitudes between experimentally produced groups: Robbers' Cave Study, cited in Sherif, M., Harvey, O.J., White, B.J., Hood, W.R. and Sherif, C.W. (1954/1961) *Study of Positive and Negative Intergroup Attitudes Between Experimentally Produced Groups: Robbers Cave Study, (10)*. Norman, OK: University Book Exchange.

www.agreatescaperoom.com

www.exitgames.co.uk and www.thelogicescapesme.com (the UK's most informative websites on the growing phenomenon)

https://www.cpdstandards.com/providers/?s=21190 (accredited Teambuilding activity link)

4.6 Emotional labour

'If your emotional abilities aren't in hand, if you don't have self-awareness, if you are not able to manage your distressing emotions, if you can't have empathy and have effective relationships, then no matter how smart you are, you are not going to get very far.'

(Daniel Goleman, 2005)

Why

It is the role of your managers to replenish your emotional store, or to contain your anxieties. However, this does not always happen. It is not advisable to expect partners or families to be the sounding board for your concerns because they do not know first-hand how you do your job. The most common response if you complain a lot about work is 'Well, just leave!' Too often you do not want to leave, but you do, however, want things to improve.

Business brief

Arlie Russell Hochschild (1983) defined emotional labour as any job that requires one to put on a bodily display of emotion that may meet the expectations of others, but is in conflict with what one is really thinking and feeling. The manager is an emotional labourer. You will need to be supportive when you may feel frustrated, or nurturing in the face of unkindness. You cannot seek your emotional support from your team, but you do need emotional support from somewhere. If you think of emotion as a sponge – and as a manager a part of your job involves containing the anxieties of your team – at some point you will need to release it or you will no longer be able to do your job effectively. Conversely, if you see emotion as a supply which keeps diminishing as you expend it, it needs to be recharged.

Try this

1. Draw a line down the middle of the gingerbread man.

2. On the left-hand side (inside the shape) write down all the things that you feel about your job – good and bad.

3. On the right-hand side (outside the shape) write down all the things you would LIKE to feel about your job.

4. On the left-hand side (outside the shape) identify the people who could help you turn the negative things (inside left) to the positive (outside right).

5. On the right-hand side (inside the shape), put together a plan of action of the things you will do to feel more positive. (No more than five things – otherwise you will become overwhelmed and not do them!)

6. Seek solace and support in colleagues – ideally those of similar status to you as they will understand your experiences and concerns. Further, you are likely to be able to help them in return!

Reflection

- How did it work?

- What will I do next time?

References

Goleman, D. (2005) *Emotional Intelligence: Why it can Matter More than IQ*. New York, NY: Bantam Books.

Hochschild, A.R. (1983) *The Managed Heart*. Berkeley and Los Angeles, CA: University of California Press.

4.7 Making meetings motivational

> *'If you had to identify, in one word, the reason why the human race has not achieved, and will never achieve, its full potential, that word would be "meetings".'*

(Dave Barry, 1999)

Why

If your own reaction to meetings is 'Oh what a waste of time', at least you are now in a position to change them. Meetings are an opportunity to meet face to face with the majority of your team, and therefore the best way to make sure information is communicated and discussed. However, they usually fail because of poor management. Many staff feel meetings are a waste of time, yet they needn't be.

Business brief

Once you have your time, venue, cakes/biscuits, agenda and attendees, you need to structure the meeting itself. First, you must ensure there is a strong chair who can keep time. Do not over- or underestimate the times stated on your agenda. What's more, USE your agenda as a working document – it's not there just for show, so stick to the times and topics!

The small points can often be worked through quickly, but there will always be areas that require a lot of discussion.

Edward de Bono (1985) used 'Thinking Hats' as a method of evaluation and analysis, and it is a system that can be applied to the more contentious meeting topics or during a 'listening event'. Each of the six hats is a different colour and is used to represent the nature of the discussion at that point in time e.g.: The white hat represents facts; the red – feelings; the black – cautions; the yellow – benefits; the green – ideas (or creativity) and the blue hat represents action (or process). The chair can use each hat to shape the discussion and move it along. The chair should time the use of each hat, and not allow hats to be merged, e.g. 'We are now moving onto the "black hat" – I would like you to raise all negative aspects surrounding the issue within the next three minutes. If you do not raise it now, you will NOT get another chance as we will move onto the next hat.'

Using hats or not, being strict with timing and explicit with your instruction that concerns should be raised now rather than later, enables the group to speak at a time when things can be done (rather than whinge later at the water cooler). Be firm on times and, in addition, empower your team to generate solutions after they have aired their feelings.

Whatever your tools to structure a meeting, the key is to remain on time and generate solutions, and a structure facilitates this.

Try this

1. If this meeting is following a previous one, make sure the minutes are circulated in good time after the original

meeting (ideally while your team can still remember what was discussed).

2. Send out your requests for agenda topics early enough for people to think about them. If there is a contentious point, make sure that you say the meeting will include it.

3. Once you have the agenda, make sure you estimate your times as accurately as possible.

4. Ask for apologies and set the date/time/venue so your team can plan.

5. See if your budget will cover refreshments – even a simple packet of biscuits can say something about your appreciation.

6. Start on time – if need be, swap minor agenda items if someone essential to one of the points is late.

7. Use the Thinking Hats or a similar tool to structure the discussion of contentious points or problems.

8. Stick to your times for each agenda point – and always allow time for solutions to be generated.

9. Thank your team for attending and ensure the minutes are typed up, approved by you and circulated for approval within two days of the meeting.

10. Action solutions generated where possible, and keep your team updated.

Reflection

- How did it work?

- What will I do next time?

References

Barry, D. (1999) *Dave Barry Turns 50.* New York, NY: Ballantine Books Inc.

de Bono, E. (1985) *Six Thinking Hats: An Essential Approach to Business Management.* New York, NY: Little, Brown, & Company.

Chapter **5**

Delegation

5.1 Make sure the task is one you CAN delegate

Delegation is a necessity. It is a way of developing your team as well as ensuring your own work is completed. The art of delegation merits a chapter to itself as new managers often struggle with it, and getting it right – or wrong – makes a great impact on staff. Successful delegation is about knowing *what* to delegate as well as *how*. Common mistakes new managers make range from one end of the spectrum (delegating too small, or too menial, a task) to the other (delegating something which should not be delegated at all). The other consideration is whether you have the personnel who actually have the skills to *do* the task. Whether you delegate a task to your team, to another department or to colleagues, the point is not to rid yourself of your responsibility for the job, but rather to formally engage others to get the job done.

Do this
Can you identify your fears about delegating? How many can you substantiate? This chapter is all about getting delegation right – so read on.

5.2 Choose the right person to delegate to

Once you have decided whether a task can, or should, be delegated, the next decision is choosing the right person for the job. Delegation is a means to develop your team, enabling them to consider the roles of management. It is a way for you to demonstrate your trust in them, as well as a means of reducing your own workload in order to concentrate on other matters. The person you choose needs to be capable of doing the task (or able to learn), and needs to be of appropriate authority depending on the nature of the task to be delegated.

Do this

List the jobs you need to delegate and the options for delegation. Match them up. (Visual representations often help clarify your thinking.)

5.3 Communicate the task effectively

Delegation is not just saying 'Here's the project, off you go'. That is not because your team won't understand the job, but rather because they may not understand exactly what you want and what your standards are – in the same way that two people may have two completely different perspectives of the same situation. Even if you are not sure what you want, if you at least know what you do *not* want, then make that clear. A little time and effort spent in explaining your expectations will make a huge difference (personally, professionally and in performance) in the long run.

You asked for a 'cake' . . . which did YOU expect?

Do this

Ask the person to whom you delegated the task to complete the form when they in turn delegate the same task to someone else.

5.4 Allow appropriate time

While you may have your concerns about the deadlines you have been given, try to protect your team from them. If you know a task will take you a certain amount of time to complete, do not expect it to be done in much less by someone else, especially if you are delegating it to someone who may have less experience than you. If you are delegating something to someone for the first time, build in 'check in' time, just in case more help is needed than you first considered. Alternatively, if someone seems to be approaching the task very confidently – for example, because they have experience that you do not – then allow them less time, but remember to check in and keep an eye on progress.

Do this

With each task you delegate, base the time frame on how long you would take to complete the task. If you are delegating the task to someone with around the same level of experience, allow them a similar amount of time. If they have less experience, allow them more time.

5.5 Offer appropriate support

'My door is always open' is not only vague, but often untrue. To get support 'just right' is hard. Set aside specific time for a face to face 'check in' on the task, and also be available for quick questions. Ask your team to prepare the questions prior to their meeting with you – not only does this ensure that everything is discussed in an efficient manner, but it is good practice of other management skills that your team can develop. Resist the temptation to solve any issues on your team's behalf, but support them, perhaps through coaching questions (see Chapter 3). If you have to intervene, then make it clear why you are doing so.

Do this

Set clear times for your team to feed back to you and keep those times free. (If no-one calls, use this time as 'team development time' to evidence their appraisals or find appropriate training courses for them.)

5.6 Let the task get done (don't micro-manage)

If intervention at an earlier point (see section 5.5) was unnecessary, and you are confident that the job will be done well, then let your team do it. There is nothing more disheartening for your team – or time wasting for you – than micro-management. Of course the task will ultimately be your responsibility, but so was the delegation of it. If you've done that correctly, the task itself should be easy to sign off.

Do this

If you feel the urge to micro-manage, visit this webpage **now**: *Open Letter to Micromanagers* by Scott Berkun (http://scottberkun.com/2009/letter-to-micromanagers/).

5.7 Delegation as a development tool (praise and appraise)

Once the task is done offer feedback to your team, and pass on any praise from higher sources. Never forget that it is no longer the 'doing' of the job that showcases your skill, but the 'getting it done'. Praise your team, keeping note of their success for the appraisal process. Find the time to debrief them on the task and ask them what they enjoyed, which areas they would like to develop in and whether they would wish for a similar opportunity should it arise. Not only are you up-skilling your workforce, but you are also encouraging your team to take an active approach to their professional development. This can only benefit future performance. Getting a job is not the end, it is the beginning – help your team navigate their path within your organisation.

Do this

If you have delegated all your tasks, you can work on your own development. Return to your three-point goal in section 1.7 and move onto point 2!

5.1 Make sure the task is one you CAN delegate

> *'You can delegate authority, but you cannot delegate responsibility'*
>
> (Byron Dorgan, cited in Maxwell, 2014)

Why

Delegation is another means of communicating within your organisation and it will be judged by your team and colleagues in the same way as your other behaviours. If you do not delegate you will not have the capacity to complete the tasks that you have, which can, in turn, negatively impact on your behaviour within the workplace. Further, you also deny yourself an opportunity to develop the skills of your team, which helps you fulfil another element of your role – moving your department forward. An organisation that is not progressing is stagnating, and appropriate delegation is one way of driving it on.

Business brief

Managers often allow their egos to prevent them from delegating and, when they realise they cannot possibly hold onto every task that needs to be done, they delegate poorly. This may be because they have assigned a task that either gives the team the impression that they are being 'stitched up' or, alternatively, is one that in reality can only be done by the manager. Having to ask for a task back after realising that it cannot be done without breaching confidentiality does not do much for your credibility.

Breaching a psychological contract through poor delegation is also a huge contributor to workplace cynicism due to the questions it raises about the integrity of the people involved (Johnson and O'Leary-Kelly, 2003), e.g. 'My job description states a commitment to developing my skills, but instead I'm writing a checklist of the items the client should have delivered.' It would be better to delegate the task of writing to the client to request the delivery checklist while agreeing a new system so the oversight does not recur. This is a more meaningful task than simply writing a list and allows negotiation skills to be developed.

Try this

If you have taken heed of the previous chapters (and in particular section 1.2), this task is quite easy – you already know what your job entails. It is therefore easy to decide which current tasks can be delegated, and assess incoming work with the same consideration.
A rule of thumb is:

- If the task contains confidential information it cannot be delegated.

- *All* other tasks can.
  - Proviso (a) to the above – always bear in mind that delegation is a development tool. If clearing out the stock cupboard is not fun for you, it certainly will not be fun for the person who could be your successor . . . on the other hand, however, 'managing the stock levels' may well be interesting.
  - Proviso (b) to the above – you will not always be delegating to your immediate team. Are other departments better placed to assist you with the task?
- Always remember delegation *develops others and supports your workload* – it should never be about passing the buck to someone else.

See delegation as a fundamental part of your job description and perfect the art.

Reflection

- How did it work?

```

```

- What will I do next time?

```

```

References

Johnson, J. and O'Leary-Kelly, A.M. (2003) The effects of psychological contract breach and organizational cynicism: not all social exchange violations are created equal, *Journal of Organizational Behavior*, 24, 627–647.

Maxwell, J.C. (2014) *Good Leaders Ask Great Questions: Your Foundation for Successful Leadership*. Nashville, TN: Center Street.

5.2 Choose the right person to delegate to

'The conventional definition of management is getting work done through people, but real management is developing people through work.'

(Agha Hasan Abedi, cited in Anderson, 2013)

Why

Delegation involves (i) getting a job done, and (ii) developing the skills of your team. When done correctly it demonstrates trust and ensures development as well as a high level of performance. Asking someone to do a task that they have already proven they can do makes sense because the work will be done quickly and done well. However, this does not progress their skills. Asking someone to do a task in which they have no experience will develop their skills, but it may take longer, and they may need extra support so as to not feel they have been 'set up to fail'. In the short term who you choose to delegate to may depend on factors such as available time and personnel, but even with those constraints, if you know your staff (and their workplace needs) and know your job, it is a highly effective way to get tasks done to a high level of performance, and will strengthen your team whilst enabling personal and departmental growth.

Business brief

This chapter starts with the presumption that you are planning on delegating – or rather, planning your delegating! Schriesheim et al. (1998) found that if a delegated task was perceived as 'dumping' it resulted in lower extrinsic satisfaction at work. In today's current job climate, there is an abundance of highly qualified graduates, but not a lot of jobs (*Bloomberg Business Insider* and multiple 2015 news reports). Therefore staff development is ever more important. However, rather than cynically developing your team so that they don't go somewhere else for a better deal, seize this opportunity to nurture this abundant talent into your own high fliers. 'Nothing engages someone like having trust placed in them . . . Trust is the most compelling form of human motivation, and delegation is a practice that demonstrates trust' (Covey, 2013). However, trust relies on you having a firm belief in the ability of the person to do the job. Trust is demonstrated by tasks that engage, not those that could be done by just about anyone. Trust entails ensuring the person you are entrusting with the task has the tools to succeed. Trust is mutual. With the potential for such empowerment, delegation should not be taken lightly.

Try this

When choosing the person/department to delegate to:

1. Be aware of the options available to you. This means considering the other departments within your organisation as well as your own team. Even if you do not use outside staff, you might be able to use their materials.

2. If you have little time available and you know your delegate is good at the task explain this to them. Then look for opportunities to develop the skills they wish to develop the next time round.

3. If you are using delegation to develop your team, be aware that you may need to offer support which means you need to have the time available to do it. If you can spare a staff member then having the learner shadow the more experienced employee may be an option. This has the added bonus of allowing the 'expert' to develop their mentoring skills within a task that they are already familiar with.

4. If you are delegating a 'menial' task acknowledge this, and try to avoid having to do so again in the future by asking the delegate to develop a better system. This will make the task more engaging, and again will allow your staff member to develop problem solving skills.

5. Remain aware of what your team wants. If a team member's wants and your needs are a close fit, delegation is where the two overlap.

Reflection

- How did it work?

- What will I do next time?

┌───┐
│   │
│   │
│   │
│   │
│   │
│   │
└───┘

References

Anderson, C. (2013) *16 Management Quotes from the Top Managers in the World,* SmartBusinessTrends.com, http://smartbusinesstrends. com/16-management-quotes/ (retrieved August 2015).

Covey, S.M.R. (2013) Podcast interview transcribed: https://www. entreleadership.com/articles/how-to-delegate#sthash.IDIIsIA4. dpuf (retrieved August 2015).

Schriesheim, C.A., Neider, L.L. and Scandura, T.A. (1998) Delegation and leader-member exchange: main effects, moderators, and measurement issues, *Academy of Management Journal,* 41(3), 298–318.

5.3 Communicate the task effectively

'Cyclops, you asked about my famous name . . . my name is Nobody.

'Polyphemus roared "Nobody is killing me, my friends" . . .

'They answered him . . . "well then, if nobody is hurting you . . . it must be sickness given by great Zeus, one you can't escape."'

(The Odyssey, Homer)

Why

The arguably overused training exercise where one person describes a picture that the other has to draw demonstrates that 'circle shaped head' (or other descriptive term) can mean one thing to one person and something very different to another. In delegating your task you need to make your expectations, standards of quality and deadlines clear. This is especially so if you have not previously delegated this particular task to anyone before or if you are delegating to a new or untried person or team. In the latter case, the person or team in question may use a process or method to complete the task that conflicts with your own. Make sure that you know what you are getting by making your wishes clear.

Business brief

Parsons (1998) states that effective delegation is highly correlated to job satisfaction and common complaints include poorly defined tasks and poor planning from the management. When faced with the unknown it is natural for people to feel apprehensive, mainly because they do not want to fail. Therefore, when delegating it is your responsibility as manager to make the *pathway* to success clear. This is only possible if you know what your desired outcome is and if the basic resources are in place to achieve it. This may include people with the correct skills, or the correct equipment. Of course people can be highly ingenious so it is possible to succeed without the latter, but if you are going to attempt this, at least make it clear beforehand that problem solving of this nature is to be part of the delegated task.

Try this

A little extra effort in the early stages of delegation can prevent problems in the later stages – when there is less time to fix them.

1. Know the outcome that you want – 'completed' is too vague a term.

2. If you do not have time to explain (and even if you do) write your list of expectations so it is easy for your delegate to refer to them.

3. If possible, give an example of the finished product or outcome.

4. Make sure you set clear boundaries. If you are happy for your delegate to take their own initiative, then let them know. If you would rather they didn't, then make that clear too.

5. Explain what materials are available for use and if innovation of any kind is required.

   NB: If the delegate does act on their own initiative or uses any type of innovative thinking or method, then be sure to acknowledge this and praise them for it.

6. Ensure your timeline (including the times for 'checking back' on progress) is unambiguous.

7. ALWAYS take time to double check if your delegate has any questions before and during the task. Establish which means of communication should be used and ensure you are available to answer any questions they may have.

Reflection

- How did it work?

- What will I do next time?

References

Homer (n.d.) *The Odyssey,* Classics.mit.edu, http://classics.mit.edu/Homer/odyssey.html (retrieved August 2015).

Parsons, L.C. (1998) Delegation skills and nurse job satisfaction, *Nursing Economics,* 16(1), 18–26.

5.4 Allow appropriate time

'If you don't have time to do it right, when will you have time to do it over?'

(John Wooden, cited in ESPN.com, 2010)

Why

Giving someone too much or too little time to do a task can damage performance. Too much and they may be tempted to wait until the last minute and rush it, too little and they may feel overwhelmed. If you have already considered the person and their level of experience along with the resources they will have at their disposal you should be able to assign a realistic time frame to the task. It is even easier if you have a frame of reference, i.e. how long the task has taken previously. The time frame required is particularly pertinent to justify if the task is supplementary to your delegate's everyday duties.

Business brief

The SMART approach to goals was defined by Doran in 1981. The acronym stands for:

- Specific
- Measurable
- Attainable
- Relevant
- Time-bound

It is time that is of interest in this chapter. The T in SMART originally stood for 'time-bound', but recent use of the acronym has often substituted the word 'timely' (e.g. Haughey, 2014). This does not create the sense of urgency that 'time-bound' does, and so is best avoided. Doran (1981) states that if a time frame is specified then the mind is already primed to consider the task, thus making your delegate more proactive in their focus. 'Timely' on the other hand suggests that as long as it is done 'in good time' everything will be fine. This defeats the purpose of having SMART-defined goals in the first place. Effective delegation does not have room for vagueness, and neither do your staff . . . or your success as a manager!

Try this

1. Be aware of the final deadline YOU need to meet.

2. Ask your delegate what they believe would be a realistic time frame within that boundary.

3. Build in extra time for a face to face check in (Use your judgment when deciding how much time to allow – you know the task, the person and their materials.)

4. Allow at least a day (more if the task is bigger) for someone who has the mind-set of a 'completer finisher' to consider the task (Belbin, 1981).

5. Never forget that you retain ultimate responsibility for the end product.

Reflection

- How did it work?

- What will I do next time?

References

Belbin, M. (1981) *Management Teams*. London: Heinemann.

Doran, G.T. (1981) There's a S.M.A.R.T. way to write management's goals and objectives, *Management Review* (AMA FORUM), 70(11), 35–36.

ESPN.com (2010) John Wooden's greatest quotes – the wizard's wisdom 'Woodenisms', *Sports.ESPN.go.com*, 5 June, http://sports.espn.go.com/ncb/news/story?id=5249709 (retrieved August 2015).

Haughey, D. (2014) *Smart Goals*, Projectsmart.co.uk, http://www.projectsmart.co.uk/smart-goals.php (retrieved July 2015).

5.5 Offer appropriate support

'My success was due to good luck, hard work, and support and advice from friends and mentors. But most importantly, it depended on me to keep trying after I had failed.'

(Mark Warner, cited in Saeks, 2010)

Why

Although one of your key duties is 'getting the job done', a skilled manager is as much a team leader as an expert on the process of completing the task. A good manager will know their team and will work with people as individuals, rather than just issuing directives. Someone new to a task will need more guidance than someone with a lot of experience; you may wish to extend the remit of more experienced staff members and delegate them more challenging tasks. Successful performance is achieved through understanding the person and their knowledge of, and ability to perform, the process. Of greatest benefit to you will be communicating with your delegate and figuring out how much guidance they will require.

Business brief

Chapman (2012) listed a set of ten levels of delegation, from 'Do as you are told', to 'Decide what action needs to be taken and manage the situation accordingly'. There is no hard and fast rule to the amount of support given on a delegated task – your job is to know the needs of your delegates, choose the most appropriate level and be prepared to adapt as you proceed. Delegation has certain similarities with situational leadership (Blanchard et al., 1985) and you must choose whether to 'Tell' (or direct the task),

'Sell' (or coach the task), get 'Participation' (merely support the task) or 'Delegate' (leave the entire task to the delegate). Be sure not to confuse this meaning of the verb 'delegate', as used in Blanchard's work, with the more general use and the way we are using it in this book, i.e. assigning all or part of a task to someone and supporting them to do the work effectively. This requires you to have a good understanding of your team. This is key to your ability to delegate successfully. Further, as delegation is about empowerment, resist the temptation to solve any problems should the delegate get stuck. Instead use coaching techniques (Chapter 3) to help them come up with solutions, while being on hand to assist with this if necessary.

Try this

1. Ask your delegate how much support they think they will need, timetable it in and review it regularly.

   NB: If your delegate thinks they will need a lot of support but you believe they need less, have the first meeting with them as scheduled, praise them for what they have achieved so far and then suggest a longer gap before the next catch-up. If you insist from the beginning that your own suggested timetable for meetings is correct, your delegate may feel undermined (and in any case you may be wrong!). If the situation is the reverse (you believe they need more support than they think they do) then an early review date is only sensible and should not be postponed.

2. Ask your delegate what support they will need and provide it.

3. Ensure you have an accessible (and monitored) means of communication should extra help be needed.

4. Use coaching questions to assist in the first instance when help is required.

Reflection

- How did it work?

```




```

- What will I do next time?

```




```

References

Blanchard, K.H., Zigarmi, P. and Zigarmi, D. (1985) *Leadership and the One Minute Manager: Increasing Effectiveness through Situational Leadership.* New York, NY: Morrow.

Chapman, A. (2012*) Delegating Authority Skills, Tasks and the Process of Effective Delegation,* Businessballs.com, www.businessballs.com/delegation.htm (retrieved July 2015),

Saeks, F. (2010) *Superpower! How to Think, Act, and Perform with Less Effort and Better Results.* Chichester: John Wiley & Sons.

5.6 Let the task get done (don't micro-manage)

> *'Even if you are 30% better at a task than someone who works for you, the time it takes for you to check on them every few hours and demand approvals over trivial decisions, costs more in morale, passion for work and destruction of self-respect among your staff than the 30% you think you're adding.'*
>
> (Scott Berkun, 2009)

Why

One of the biggest complaints from staff is that they do not feel trusted to do the jobs they have been asked to do. If you have chosen your delegate correctly, and you have allowed sufficient time and offered the appropriate support, why *are* you still involved in the task? Why are you not using your (now freed up) time to complete your other work, or starting to move your department forward? The point of delegation is not doing the task yourself. If you are hanging onto the task you need to ask yourself why.

Business brief

Our own fear of failure, classified as a specific phobia in the DSM IV (APA, 1994), can often result in us sticking to tasks we know we can do. Vygotsky's (1978) theory of learning suggests that people learn through the guidance of a 'more knowledgable other' (MKO) who can support the learner from the known to the unknown. In the case of delegation and your team, the MKO is you. But what about when it's just you? Unfortunately managers don't always have someone looking out for them, so you need to be your own guide. If you are aware that you are micro-managing, ask yourself 'Why am I doing this?' If the answer is 'Because my delegate is failing' then readdress sections 1–5 in this chapter. If it is 'Because I don't want to let go', cut those strings – you're a manager now!

Try this

1. Always bear in mind your skills set is focused on 'co-ordinating the process' not 'doing' it. Your abilities are assessed according to *how well* you have delegated.

2. Ask yourself why you are micro-managing and take steps to solve it.

3. Read the rest of Scott Berkun's *Open Letter to Micro-managers* and ask yourself how you would feel if you were the person being micro-managed.

4. Identify what your fears are about the job – see if they can be addressed without the need for micro-managing.

Reflection

- How did it work?

- What will I do next time?

References

American Psychiatric Association (APA) (1994) *Diagnostic and Statis-
   tical Manual of Mental Disorders,* 4th edn. Washington, DC: APA.
Berkun, S. (2009) *An Open Letter to Micromanagers,* Scottberkun.
   com, http://scottberkun.com/2009/letter-to-micromanagers/
   (retrieved August 2015).
Vygotsky L.S (1978), *Mind in Society: Development of Higher Psychological Processes,* Cambridge, MA: Harvard University Press.

5.7 Delegation as a development tool (praise and appraise)

'Our work is our most important resource to develop our people.'

(Jim Trinka and Les Wallace, 2015)

Why

Recognising and praising the efforts of your team reinforces the knowledge that you had trust in them and they came through for you. This will give them confidence in future tasks. In addition, it means that as you pass more of your work onto them, you can acquire new work for yourself. You are developing your staff, and they in turn are allowing you the freedom to develop yourself and your department. Praise and recognition can be given immediately and in an informal manner; they can also be given more formally through the appraisal process. The latter is important because it is a chance to put on the record what your staff have been able to achieve. When you do so, take care to be specific with your congratulations.

Business brief

Halvorson (2011) in the *Harvard Business Review* said one of the most effective ways to become more successful is to be specific with our goals. If your delegates have succeeded in planning and executing an event for 300 people, be specific when praising them – it will sound a lot better than 'they hosted a nice party'. We are not very good at being specific at defining our goals, perhaps because we do not always know what we want, but when a goal has been achieved it is easy to break down each element and frame it as a skill that has been attained. Your praise following the successful completion of a clearly delegated task should be specific and involve quantification and, if necessary, comparison. It is good practice for you to do this as a manager as your team may not be as good at doing it themselves. Quantifying and praising exactly what has been achieved addresses both the delegate who is too modest as well as the one who is too arrogant.

Try this

1. Informally praise successes as you see them

2. Formally break down what has been done and include it as skills attained in your staff member's next appraisal.

3. Ask them what they would like to develop further and look for opportunities to progress this.

4. Implement those opportunities and update your team's TNA/appraisal form.

Reflection

- How did it work?

- What will I do next time?

```
┌──────────────────────────────────────────────┐
│                                                │
│                                                │
│                                                │
│                                                │
│                                                │
└──────────────────────────────────────────────┘
```

References

Halvorson, H.G. (2011) Nine things successful people do differently, *HBR.org*, http://hbr.org/2011/02/nine-things-successful-people (retrieved July 2015).

Trinka, J. and Wallace, L. (2015) *Leadership Quotes,* Govleaders.org, http://govleaders.org/quotes.htm (retrieved August 2015).

Chapter **6**

Troubleshooting

6.1 Responding to a complaint

Prevention is always better than cure, but inevitably you will need to deal with complaints. These can stem from within your team, or from your client base. See the complaint as an opportunity – the complainant chose to talk to you first instead of voting with their feet. While it is never pleasant to receive criticism, how you respond can retain, gain or lose loyal custom. Knee-jerk reactions are often not appropriate and being too quick to change something following a singular complaint may risk upsetting others. When dealing with complaints remain calm and open minded and treat the process as an investigation.

Do this
Next time you receive a complaint, extract the FACTS and start investigating from there.

6.2 Investigating a complaint

When investigating a complaint start from a neutral standpoint, and if you cannot do that, ask someone else to investigate or go over your findings with you. Employing a technique such as the '5 Whys' is useful in getting to the root of the complaint. Fixing the issue at the root will be more effective than managing the symptoms as it will prevent recurrence.

Do this

If, during your investigation, you ask 'Why?' and the reply is 'I don't know', take a leaf from coaching (section 3.2) and say 'Imagine if you did'.

6.3 Don't go it alone (but be discerning about who you involve)

If you need support with your investigation, or if the investigation reveals something that you are not sure how to address, seek support from other management colleagues or your Human Resources (HR) department. Don't allow your pride to compromise an already delicate situation. Ask for help if you need it, but remember to involve the appropriate people. Not only is turning an investigation into organisational grapevine fodder embarrassing for those involved, but it can cause you problems on the legal front as well.

Do this

Identify who you know that could help you with an investigation. Keep this list handy.

6.4 Managing challenging conversations

If a challenging conversation needs to happen, have it as soon as possible before the issue requires more than just a conversation. Be sure of your facts, and bring in a neutral person (such as a member of HR) if you feel that you will be affected emotionally. Allow the person with whom you are having the conversation to bring someone as well. Arrange a convenient time for all parties at a neutral place, and follow the simple steps within the 'Big picture' section.

Do this

Refer to the list you just made (section 6.3). Could any of those people be your 'neutral'?

6.5 Whistleblowing

If your team or your clients cannot talk to you, make sure they can talk to someone – and someone who isn't the media. Anonymous feedback or suggestion boxes (that people know exist!) are a way of encouraging a climate of reporting especially when there is a huge emphasis placed on meeting targets. It takes a lot of courage for someone to speak out against an organisational culture. However incredulous you may be, take the act seriously. A genuine injustice will come out no matter how much you try to hide it – don't let cover-ups be at the expense of people!

Do this

Read your whistleblowing policy, and make sure your team know who they can talk to – if not to you.

6.6 Managing the organisational grapevine

The organisational grapevine has its benefits, as long as you take the rumours with a pinch of salt. However, if you hear discussion about something under your control the best plan is to address the issue by being open and transparent. Communicate. It is always better that information comes from YOU as you know it is accurate. (But it never hurts to hear what the gossip is either. Don't add to it, but be aware you may need to correct it!)

Do this

Think back to the last thing you heard on the organisational grapevine – who was it from and how much of it was true? Bear this in mind for future rumours.

6.7 Dealing with bad publicity

It is always a shame when a complaint finds its way into the public domain – but with the amount of review sites available online it is almost inevitable. Do not get drawn into an argument – address the complaint when you find out about it, investigate it and respond to the facts in an explanatory rather than a defensive manner. If there are complete untruths or clear misunderstandings within the statement present these from your point of view and offer to make amends within your remit. Try to speak to the person directly as a genuine complainant may have suggestions for improvement but, again, do so with a neutral observer. Don't forget that sometimes people just enjoy complaining and an unfounded complaint may need to be described as such.

Do this
Try NOT to google yourself!

6.1 Responding to a complaint

'You can't heal what you don't acknowledge.'

(Jack Canfield, in Minow, 2012)

Why

A genuine complaint can be seen as receiving an opportunity to make amends. Rather than ignoring the problem and moving their custom, or, in the case of a member of staff, leaving the company, the complainant has given you an opportunity to right the perceived wrong. Even if you are unable to address the complaint in full immediately, show your appreciation by acknowledging receipt at once. Feeling unheard can be frustrating, and the longer it goes on, the more time you are leaving for the complainant to create scenarios in their head – most of them unpleasant for you.

Business brief

'Complaining is hard to avoid, but try to do it with a purpose,' writes Alina Tugend (2013) in *The New York Times*. The best type of complaint foregoes the 'whiney, entitled air' (Bowen, 2013) and is clear about the desired solution. Those are the type of complaints to treasure because they not only move you to act, but also indicate what you can do to please the complainant. Unfortunately, the purpose of most complaints is to vent rather than rectify (Tugend, 2013), but that doesn't mean you respond any differently. Thank the person for bringing it to your attention (note that sometimes complaints are indirect, e.g. 'I'm a bit warm' rather than 'Can you turn off the heating, please?'), and act on it. Investigate, conclude and report back. Meanwhile, also try to encourage your staff to be specific with their complaints or concerns.

Try this

1. Always acknowledge receipt of a complaint, and if you cannot respond directly, state exactly when the complainant will receive their response. (This may be directed by your policies, but good practice is within 14 days.)

2. Begin your investigation ensuring you seek only to discuss the facts of the matter.

3. Produce your report and response in a timely manner – bearing in mind that you may need to show your response to those you have spoken to within the investigation before sending it to the complainant.

4. If the complaint is unfounded, be clear in your reasons why and signpost the complainant with regards to taking the matter further.

5. Make sure you have documented your process according to your 'dealing with complaints' procedure.

Reflection

- How did it work?

- What will I do next time?

References

Bowen, W. (2013) *A Complaint Free World,* Will Bowen.com, http://www.acomplaintfreeworld.org/ (retrieved September 2015).

Minow, N. (2012) Interview: 'Chicken Soup's' Jack Canfield about his new book on tapping into ultimate success, *beliefnet,* August, http://www.beliefnet.com/columnists/moviemom/2012/08/interview-chicken-soups-jack-canfield-about-his-new-book-on-tapping-into-ultimate-success.html (retrieved September 2015).

Tugend, A. (2013) Complaining is hard to avoid, but try to do it with a purpose, *The New York Times,* 3 May, http://www.nytimes.com/2013/05/04/your-money/the-satisfaction-and-annoy-ance-of-complaining.html (retrieved September 2015).

6.2 Investigating a complaint

> *'This act of complaining ... is a symptom not the disease itself. Just as the severity of a medical complaint should be measured not by how loudly it draws attention to itself but by the extent to which the body is really damaged, so we should not mistake the loudness of a complaint for its seriousness.'*
>
> (Julian Baggini, 2008)

Why

The act of investigating is fraught with emotion. Whether valid or not, complaints immediately trigger a feeling of defensiveness. If you, or others, are in a position of defensiveness, this hinders finding out if there really is a problem that needs to be addressed. If you can remove the emotion – from your own perception as well as those you wish to involve in your investigation – you will make better progress in identifying the facts and solving the problem.

Business brief

Baggini (2008) advises that the act of complaining or 'just saying/ observing/other-polite-means-of-raising-the-point' occurs when the person moved to speak feel that things are not as they 'should be'. However, the way that the complainant chooses to express themselves may vary according to their perception of the event, their communication preferences and what the act of complaining means to them. For Baggini, some people 'are never happier than when they get the chance to complain, while others are deeply unhappy . . . but just accept it'. The fact that a complaint has arrived means you need to investigate it, and do your best to see through the surrounding 'white noise'.

Root cause analysis is a technique used widely within engineering which offers a structured, and unemotional, approach to investigation. It usually includes five steps:

Step 1.   Define the problem

Step 2.   Collect data and information about the problem

Step 3.   Identify all possible causes of the problem

Step 4.   Based on the above, identify the root cause – the singular cause that gave rise to everything else

Step 5.   Recommend and implement solutions for tackling the problem at the root.

(Mindtools, Root Cause Analysis, 2015)

Using these steps will enable you to structure a full explanation of your findings and what you intend to do which you can then feed back to the complainant.

Try this

When you receive a complaint:

1. Acknowledge receipt at once and give a reasonable time frame for your response.

2. Try to remove the emotion from the situation by listing the facts of the case.

3. Once you have the facts present them to the relevant parties, making time for a meeting with them if necessary. Be sure you do not assign blame – every party to the investigation must feel that this is simply fact-finding.

4. If necessary remind each party of the need for confidentiality.

5. Use root cause analysis techniques – e.g. explore the responses given by each person by using the '5 Whys' (i.e. asking 'Why?' five times).

6. Collaborate to find solutions.

7. Frame your response to the complainant with an explanation of why the issue occurred and what you are going to do about it.

8. If appropriate allow the parties to the investigation, as well as HR, to see your response before you send it, and make sure you do so within the time frame set.

Reflection

- How did it work?

- What will I do next time?

References

Baggini, J. (2008) *Complaint: From Minor Moans to Principled Protests*. London: Profile Books.

Mindtools (2015) *Root Cause Analysis*, Mindtools.com, http://www.mindtools.com/pages/article/newTMC_80.htm (retrieved August 2015).

6.3 Don't go it alone (but be discerning about who you involve)

'Schadenfreude: a feeling of pleasure or satisfaction when something bad happens to someone else.'

(Cambridge Dictionaries Online, 2015)

Why

It is important to involve others in your investigation. These include the people to whom you are speaking directly (or those whom you are investigating), as well as one or more members of HR, a line manager or, if appropriate, a union representative. It is important that you stress the importance of discretion and remind everyone involved of company policy on confidentiality during investigations. Discretion is essential because investigations can be embarrassing for those involved – especially if they involve a suspension. Further, it is a natural reaction to feel relief (if not pleasure and satisfaction) at someone else being the subject of a complaint and not you. This can lead to gossip and must be carefully managed.

Business brief

As part of your investigation, you may need to request employee files from HR, seek advice from a union or even ask a union

representative to attend any necessary meetings. It is worth reminding everyone concerned of the need for discretion, especially when bringing members of your own team into the investigation. Gossiping about something confidential may be seen as a human need: 'Gossip builds social bonds because shared dislikes create stronger bonds than shared positives' (Gueret, 2011). Therefore, whenever someone knows something that others do not, it may be tempting for them to wield this power in order to manipulate social bonds to their own advantage. While gossip may not in itself be harmful, it can provide evidence of harassment or discrimination, it can be detrimental to the investigation and it is also unproductive (West Virginia Employment Law Letter, 2008). Always make sure to remind your team of the need for professionalism and discretion.

Try this

1. Ensure your investigation occurs in a private setting and that all records are kept confidential.

2. Remind those involved of the need for discretion.

3. Reassure those you speak to that this is an investigative process and not a witch hunt.

4. Be aware of exactly who you have involved in the investigation so you know who to meet with if word spreads.

5. Should word get out, it is best to call a meeting with everyone, explain the negative impact of gossip and outline the consequences should it continue. This does not mean that you should threaten your team. Rather, explain to them the risks of the whole department becoming accountable simply for having engaged in idle chatter.

Reflection

- How did it work?

- What will I do next time?

References

Cambridge Dictionaries Online (2015), http://dictionary.cambridge.
  org/dictionary/english/schadenfreude (retrieved August 2015).
Gueret, C. (2011) Why we love to gossip, *Psychologies Magazine,*
  December, https://www.psychologies.co.uk/self/why-we-love-
  to-gossip.html (retrieved August 2015).
West Virginia Employment Law Letter (2008) What can HR do about
  workplace gossip?, *HR Hero Line,* 4 April, http://www.hrhero.
  com/hl/articles/2008/04/04/what-can-hr-do-about-workplace-
  gossip/ (retrieved August 2015).

6.4 Managing challenging conversations

'The single most important thing [you can do] is to shift [your] internal stance from "I understand" to "Help me understand". Everything else follows from that.'

(Patton et al., 2000)

Why

As with the section on responding to a complaint in a timely manner, if a conversation needs to happen and it is put off, the matter can escalate. Similarly to investigations, the secret to managing a difficult conversation is to manage the emotional impact on you and those with whom you are having the conversation.

Business brief

In the first instance, ACAS (Advisory, Conciliation and Arbitration Service) prefers to reframe the term 'difficult' as 'challenging'. They emphasise the importance of remaining in control of your emotions and the situation in order to address the matter and generate solutions so that all parties may move forward positively.

They offer excellent guidance in easy-to-follow downloadable handouts for a number of workplace scenarios including 'challenging conversations'. In summary they propose a focus on:

1. Facing the problem
2. Containing the problem
3. Remaining in control of the problem

(ACAS, 2014)

In facing the problem, you first must be sure that you are the right person either to deal with the matter or escalate it if not. What will help is your knowledge of any relevant HR procedures and policies and not being afraid to seek support if necessary. You need to deal with the issue in a timely manner communicating with all relevant parties along the way.

The key is to remove the fear of 'challenging conversations' by focusing on the facts and working with the parties to generate a solution.

To contain it, remain discreet and professional and ensure that records are made and kept accurately and confidentially. To remain in control, seek support from HR, as well as reflect on your own emotional concerns with regards to undertaking challenging conversations.

Try this

1. Acknowledge that difficult (or challenging) conversations are part of your working life, and reflect on your reasons for worrying about them.
2. Arrange a time and private venue for the conversation that are convenient for all parties concerned.
3. If necessary ask someone neutral to be present when you have a challenging conversation, and allow the other party or parties to be accompanied by someone they trust too. Ask for feedback and observations on your performance.

4. Always open with the facts of the issue – and stick with them. Exploring the facts may reveal other issues that need to be addressed but again, make sure it is the facts that you record for further investigation.

5. Plan your conversation so that all points you need to cover are covered.

6. Seek solutions from the parties to the conversation – try not to focus on getting your ideas accepted as your perspective may differ from that of the people directly involved.

7. Implement the solutions and monitor them for success – praising the new status quo.

Reflection

- How did it work?

- What will I do next time?

References

ACAS (2014) *Challenging Conversations and How to Manage Them,* ACAS.org.uk, http://www.acas.org.uk/media/pdf/0/d/Challenging-conversations-and-how-to-manage-them.pdf (retrieved August 2015).

Patton, B., Stone, D. and Heen, S. (2000) *Difficult Conversations: How to Discuss What Matters Most.* Harmondsworth: Penguin.

6.5 Whistleblowing

'One thing I learned as a journalist is that there is at least one disgruntled person in every workplace . . . and at least double that number with a conscience.'

(Michael Moore, 2011)

Why

Whistleblowing can be categorised as 'internal' – reporting suspected misdemeanours within the organisation – or 'external' – reporting the same to the press or other public bodies. Organisations, of course, much prefer internal whistleblowing. The only way to encourage reporting is to create a culture where people are free to talk without fear of reprisal. People often do not feel at liberty to talk because the simple act of reporting something can sometimes result in a black mark against the person who made the report. This is when you need to ask yourself what value you place on the truth.

Business brief

Whistleblowing can conjure up a wealth of emotions. It can be perceived as a betrayal, with the whistleblower a traitor to the organisation, rather than as an essential act for the greater good (Larmer, 1992). The fear of reprisal is great, and the media is quick to publish stories of whistleblowers who have faced persecution in the workplace. Rowe (1993) found that staff were more likely to report wrongdoing if there was a choice of confidential methods.

Suggestion boxes, automated software (where forms are uploaded and processed by a complaints team rather than the line manager) or someone outside the department with a link to HR are just some of those options. It is important to ensure all your team recognise that you do not condone unethical behaviour, but until you know about it, you cannot respond. Maintaining open dialogue is better than placing a great weight on blowing the whistle.

Try this

1. Continue to state your values and make it clear that (even if reporting affects targets) you would rather be made aware of issues than not.

2. Encourage your team to raise any concerns even if they end up unfounded.

3. Be extra aware when sentences begin 'This probably sounds silly . . .'.

4. If investigation is not merited, take the time to explain to the person raising the concern why this is the case, and take steps to avoid that misunderstanding from recurring.

5. Should there be a number of reports, act on them by carrying out root cause analysis in order to identify the root of the

problem and generate meaningful solutions which you must then implement.

6. Familiarise yourself with the number of methods that your staff can use if they are unhappy and cannot speak with you about the issue.

7. Remind staff that even though the initial contact may be confidential, when the issue is investigated, those involved will have a right to know who raised it in the first instance. However, ensure them that there will be no reprisals – and make sure this turns out to be the case.

Reflection

- How did it work?

- What will I do next time?

References

Larmer, R.A. (1992) Whistleblowing and employee loyalty, *Journal of Business Ethics,* 11(2), 125–128.

Moore, M. (2011) *Here Comes Trouble.* New York, NY: Grand Central Publishing.

Rowe, M. (1993) Options and choice for conflict resolution in the workplace, in Hall, L. (ed.) *Negotiation: Strategies for Mutual Gain.* Newbury Park, CA: Sage Publications, Inc., pp. 105–121.

6.6 Managing the organisational grapevine

'Gossip, as usual, was one-third right and two-thirds wrong.'
(L.M. Montgomery, 1988)

Why

As discussed in section 6.3, while gossip is something that is regularly engaged in, it is not productive and can result in negative consequences. However, especially in larger organisations, the grapevine is a useful companion to the more formal channels of communication. Although flavoured by perception and opinion, news travels much faster through the grapevine than by any other method. There is no preventing it, but it is wise for you to take the information you hear with a pinch of salt and advise your team to do the same.

Business brief

Lorette (2015) says that the 'grapevine allows feelings to be expressed instead of bottled up. People need to talk about what is affecting them . . . If managers can tap into the grapevine, they can learn a substantial amount about the issues and problems of their employees.' Use the grapevine as a starting point for open dialogue with your team about any issues they may be having. Lorette (2015) goes on to say that much of the information on the grapevine is true but may be skewed. Think of the grapevine as the Mogwai – embrace it, but do not always believe it . . . and certainly do not feed it after midnight.

Try this

1. Explain to your team that you are aware of the organisational grapevine, but remind them that information is likely to be unreliable. If they are concerned about anything they hear, encourage them to speak to you about it.

2. If there is a rumour that needs to be addressed do so as quickly and as openly as possible – ideally with your whole team. Make sure that any follow-up information, or a summary given later to anyone not present at the time, comes directly from you or else the sense may get twisted in transmission.

3. If you hear something on the grapevine that you think is a matter of concern, raise it with the people involved and explain how you heard it. If they do not know they are the subject of gossip, they may be pleased with the heads up.

4. Do not spread anything that you hear on the grapevine!

Reflection

- How did it work?

- What will I do next time?

References

Lorette, K. (2015) The importance of the organisational grapevine in internal business communications, *Small Business Chron,* http://smallbusiness.chron.com/importance-grapevine-internal-business-communications-429.html (retrieved August 2015).

Montgomery, L.M. (1990) *Chronicles of Avonlea.* London: Bantam Books.

6.7 Dealing with bad publicity

'Above all, to thine own self be true.'
(William Shakespeare, Hamlet, Act 1, Scene 3)

Why

Thanks especially to the internet, bad publicity – true or not – can spread quickly and easily, and can damage your business or reputation within seconds. The most important weapon you can use is communication. Address each complaint through a focus on the facts. If the criticism is unfounded, say so. Most importantly, remember that no matter how reasoned your approach and how valid your explanation, with the reach of the internet, someone is likely to take umbrage. As long as you feel that your integrity has not been compromised, there is no more you can do.

Business brief

The service recovery paradox is a business phenomenon where if a client or customer perceives a service error to be minor and/or not directly attributable to the organisation, and the organisation is able to deal with it, then the loyalty of that client or customer is *greater* than if the error had not occurred (Magnini et al., 2007). Therefore, not only is it right to address complaints professionally, but there is benefit in doing so as well.

195

Try this

1. Before responding, check the facts. If there are inaccuracies, contact the person who reported the situation and make this clear – but do not discuss anything further.

2. Respond as soon as possible to present a public statement that answers all issues raised.

3. Make sure that your own HR and management are aware of the situation and support your actions.

4. Make sure that your team does not speak to the press without your permission.

5. If an apology is needed, make one (note that you may need to exclude accepting liability).

6. If a criticism is unfounded explain why, but do so openly with evidence rather than defensively with attitude.

7. If appropriate and within your remit, offer to make amends.

8. Show that you have learned from the situation and state the steps being taken to rectify the situation and measures implemented to make sure it does not occur again.

9. If possible take steps so that new good publicity outshines the bad.

DO NOT:

- Go on an internet rant venting your frustrations IN CAPS!

- Reply to social media posts with anything other than the official statement or 'no comment' – you will never win over everyone and will risk saying something detrimental if you become riled.

- Google yourself for a while as you are bound to find something that prompts the two points above.

- Over-think the situation – if you have done everything you can, and retained your integrity, you will soon be 'old news' as people move onto the next story.

Reflection

- How did it work?

- What will I do next time?

```

```

References

Magnini, V.P., Ford, J.B., Markowski, E.P. and Honeycutt Jr, E.D. (2007) The service recovery paradox: justifiable theory or smoldering myth? *Journal of Services Marketing,* 21(3), 213–225.

Shakespeare, W. (1985) *Hamlet, Prince of Denmark,* ed. Edwards, P., New Cambridge Shakespeare. Cambridge: Cambridge University Press.

Afterword – Chapter 6

Bear in mind that in the aftermath of any complaint, the important thing is to re-settle your team. Your staff must know that the organisation has their best interests at heart and will always work to support them.

Chapter 7

Business ethics and integrity

7.1 The values-led organisation

A mission statement is a pledge of greatness, e.g. 'If you join our organisation we will . . . ' – and why not? Without a goal how would you know what success looks like? However, this says little about how you are going to get there. Many organisations are now moving towards being 'values-led' and it is not uncommon to see words like 'Integrity', 'Communication' or 'Excellence' featuring on every organisational touchpoint. More important than listing values is *living* them, and that is where organisations can fail. It is essential for every organisation to identify with their values to allow them to be assimilated into everyday performance.

Do this

If you were to write down three values that described your organisation's practices, what would they be? Is that a good thing? If not, identify what you can change to make them positive.

7.2 Profit v. organisational well-being

A business needs to make a profit because that is the only way it is able to survive. However, it is counter-productive to aim for this at the expense of your staff. If you reduce your team and ask them to compensate for the areas you have downsized, you will soon be left with a staff with no strength – nor desire – to work. The fear of redundancy along with the loss of friends and colleagues can have a detrimental effect on your team. Any profit that is made (or saved) will be short term as your business will not be healthy enough to continue to grow. If you need to make

human resource cuts, be specific in your decisions and look to performance rather than job role – streamline correctly and your team may even thank you. Do it wrongly, and your organisation will struggle to survive.

Do this

Identify who works well and who is in need of support. Give this support with the help of SMART action plans.

7.3 Maintaining quality

When you are asking staff to work with less support and fewer resources, quality will always be compromised. While you may be making savings in the short term, can you afford the cost of rebuilding a brand after a major service failure?

Do this

Ask yourself – do I have any quality concerns? If you do, then raise them!

7.4 Being responsible

Corporate social responsibility is another phrase that is commonly seen on corporate touchpoints. Organisations are quick to display their badges of honour (e.g. investors in people, gold standards etc.) and of course this is attractive to new recruits. However, once again, surface without substance is soon unmasked. It is now not enough to ensure your investments – and your clients – are ethical, and that you are not contributing too greatly to the carbon footprint, nor to wastage of any raw materials, but, as with the organisation's values, you have to be seen to be living in a responsible manner. With the speed at which questionable practices can be publicised via social media, responsibility cannot be taken lightly.

Do this

What have you done that's socially responsible? Tweet it!

7.5 Mad, bad, sad – treating a toxic organisation

Robinson (2009) proposes that in the same way as people can be afflicted with an illness, so too can an organisation. A sick organisation will impact on its own propensity for growth and performance. While often seen in entrepreneurial firms, where the 'character' of the organisation is shaped by the CEO, larger organisations may also become sick due to established culture and practice. How healthy are you?

Do this

Does your organisation have a high turnover? See if you can identify why – and outline a way to address it. Put forward your suggestions to your own managers.

7.6 Ethics in a globalised world

With the presence of the internet, the world is ever smaller. However, just because you come into contact with global organisations, it does not mean your practices will converge. The cultures within which many organisations operate will differ from yours due to the laws and regulations within the country. There will be workplace practices that may be unacceptable to some organisations but expected in others. You need to be able to navigate a world whose reach is growing, but whose individual cultures will need time to change.

Do this

Identify which ethical standards your organisation stands by. Tweet about those too!

7.7 Be proactive

You are a great manager – you are reading this book which means you want to learn and develop, and that alone is a positive trait. Management is to the employee as university is to the A-level student. There is no longer anyone telling you what to do. You will get help if you ask, but its quality will vary. You need to take responsibility for things which you may never have done before, and may end up doing things which you thought you had left behind many years ago. This isn't a rule book, it's a pick 'n' mix of ideas and concepts which you can use, develop, and mix and match. Choose whichever you like, use whichever you like – the more you have, the wider your choice.

No two organisations will be the same to manage, no two managers will be alike in their approach and no two books will give you the same advice. However, what is a constant is the fact that the good manager gets the job done through the collaboration of their team – the better the collaboration, the better the result. But the world is dynamic and will continue to change, so you must continue to reflect on your actions, adapting them as necessary. You have approximately six months before you become a part of the organisational culture, so use that time wisely to instigate change if necessary (or possible), and try to remain proactive in your thinking. Management is active as much as responsive; take it as a ride, not as a journey.

Do this
Chat with like-minded people, share ideas and good practices. Learn from each other. Go to http://businessmatters. freeforums.net/ and start a discussion.

BIG PICTURE
7. Business ethics and integrity

7.1 The values-led organisation

'Our values are not just words on a page – they are in our DNA. They underpin everything we do and are reflected in the day-to-day behaviour of the company.'

(Diageo, cited in Great Place to Work, 2014)

Why

Many organisations are able to establish their vision but do not consider the reality of the collateral damage that has been sustained on the way there. Being values-led focuses attention onto behaviour as the excuse of 'the end justifies the means' is removed. When you are bound by values, the *means* is the yardstick by which you will be judged. Values must be lived, not

just espoused. While you may choose your values, or they may be pre-existing, the most accurate description of what is being 'lived' comes from the staff members themselves. Your team experience the organisational culture on a day-to-day basis, so the wise manager will check in with their views from time to time.

Business brief

A 'values-led business is based on the idea that business has a responsibility to the people and the society that make its existence possible' (Cohen and Greenfield, 1997). A survey conducted by the Great Place to Work Institute found that of the top 100 organisations on the UK's 'Best Workplace' list, 97 per cent were values-led. However, their research also found that each value must be clearly defined with examples of the behaviour expected (Great Place to Work, 2014). In addition, if managers are perceived to be breaching these values, then trust will be lost, which in turn has an effect on performance and turnover. A lack of transparency behind decisions taken is the cause of some perceived breaches (Great Place to Work, 2014), but it is also notable that in larger companies, values can become 'lost in translation' if efforts are not made to define and reinforce them (Sunley, cited in Cooper, 2015).

Always be aware of the values you personally uphold and seek to engage with them in your daily working life. Even without

organisational directives, ethical behaviour is embedded in ethical people.

Try this

1. Whether you are values-led or not, ask your team to come up with the values that they believe the organisation embodies. If you are surprised (or shocked), at least you know and have the option to work to change them!

2. Ask your team what sort of values they would want to stand by and what changes they would suggest in terms of how your organisation conducts itself.

3. Ask your customers/clients what values they perceive the organisation stands for, and what values they would like you to embody.

4. If a breach has occurred investigate why it has been perceived as such and offer an explanation.

5. If you are a smaller organisation, take care to continue to reinforce and define your values as you grow.

6. Always be mindful that values need to be embodied, not just vocalised.

Reflection

- How did it work?

- What will I do next time?

```

```

References

Cohen, B. and Greenfield, J. (1997) *Ben & Jerry's Double Dip.* New York, NY: Fireside.

Cooper, N. (2015) *Leadership Disconnect v's Values-led Organisations,* changeboard.com, http://www.purplecubed.com/images/uploads/Changeboard%201(1).pdf (retrieved September 2015).

Great Place to Work (2014) *Institute Research Paper,* Greatplacetowork.co.uk, http://www.greatplacetowork.co.uk/storage/documents/organisational%20values%20are%20they%20worth%20the%20bother%20final2%20web%20031114.pdf (retrieved September 2015).

7.2 Profit v. organisational well-being

'If your conduct is determined solely by considerations of profit you will arouse great resentment.'

(Confucius)

Why

With organisations such as the National Health Service tendering for business, and educational establishments opting to raise their tuition fees, money is a bigger issue than ever. Your organisation needs to be financially sustainable but the common option seems to be reducing staff and expecting those who remain to compensate. As a worker you know this is not feasible – what makes you think it is as a manager?

Business brief

Many European firms are starting to implement 'no emails after 6' or other policies to allow their staff to take a break from work but, in contrast, in the UK managers are still working longer hours than ever (Stevens, 2011). Hollinshead et al. (1999) suggested that this is due to organisational downsizing coupled with an inability to 'distinguish fat from muscle', a view which is not often voiced, but is arguably highly relevant today. Of course a blanket approach of 'cutting jobs to save money' is inappropriate, but there will always be members of staff who work neither hard nor effectively – and often they can be identified by other team members. If you are not discerning enough when you are forced to make difficult decisions regarding redundancies your strongest workers are likely to take what's offered because they will easily walk into another job, leaving you with the dead weight – and working after 6pm. With few hard-working staff members remaining, you will be left with a 'depressed' organisation which is unable to respond to any opportunities for growth (Hollinshead et al., 1999). The good manager must identify and maximise positive contributions while dealing swiftly with those who have a negative effect on the organisation.

Try this

1. Draw a grid with skills that you need from your team on the horizontal and the names of your team members on the vertical. Mark off their skills by ticking the relevant boxes. It

is often obvious that one person is not pulling their weight in a certain area, but by making your thought process more objective, you will be able to see if they are in fact contributing somewhere else. *(NB: Do not allow your team to become aware of this. They may have their suspicions but these become harder to ignore in the face of evidence.)*

2. If someone is not contributing then speak with them and give them the opportunity to do so. Ask them if there is anything that you can do to support them better.

3. If necessary make it clear that there will be consequences if they are unable to improve their performance. Offer them the opportunity to change their working remit if possible.

4. Put in an action plan to support them (ideally worked out with them – see section 2.4 on dealing with disputes and problems) and check their progress, acknowledging if improvements are made, and following through on the consequences if not.

5. Engage your staff in generating solutions that do not involve human resource cuts.

Reflection

- How did it work?

- What will I do next time?

References

Confucius (n.d.) www.revolutionalminds.com/confuciusquotes/ (retrieved September 2015).

Hollinshead, G., Nicholls, P. and Tailby, S. (1999) *Employee Relations: A Contemporary Perspective*. Harlow: Financial Times/Prentice Hall.

Stevens, M. (2011), British staff work more hours than the European average, CIPD.co.uk, www.cipd.co.uk/pm/peoplemanagement/b/ weblog/archive/2011/12/08/british-staff-work-more-hours-than-european-average-says-ons-2011-12.aspx (retrieved Jan 2016).

7.3 Maintaining quality

'Quality means doing it right when no-one is looking.'
(Henry Ford, cited in Anderson, 2013)

Why

Whilst many people realise that blanket cuts are not the answer to sustainability, few can think of an alternative, and even fewer strive to implement it should they come up with one. The last section discussed how cuts need to be well-judged, and the astute manager will seek advice from the staff:

'If I had to save money in my department, I'd do it through being stricter on waste. We waste so much and sometimes things go in the wrong bins. The staff are a bit blasé about it, but I suppose if I told them that it was either save here, or lose a team member, they'd all do it.'

(Team Leader, NHS).

However, it takes a very strong-minded person to stand firm when their job could be on the line, but a short-term decision will have implications for long-term gain – make sure those decisions are positive.

Business brief

'False economy' is defined by the *Cambridge Dictionary* as 'an action that saves money at the beginning but, over a longer period of time, results in more money being wasted than saved'. If you cut human resources but do not have the staff to complete the job (or have overworked staff signed off sick) you will spend more in hiring and training new, less experienced staff. Similarly, if you cut the quality of materials and then have to recall a product or, worse, pay hefty compensation should someone suffer damage or injury through using it, your business will find it hard to survive. Of course there is a mentality that says 'I won't be here to see the consequences', but that is not the thought process of a good manager – and if you are thinking that, it might be in the best interests of everyone if you resign. Have the integrity to do the right thing, even in the face of adversity.

Try this

1. Involve your team in a periodic cost-audit where you can examine what is being spent and how your department can be more efficient. Remember that efficient stock taking or ordering practices as well as saving on waste can make a huge difference to budget.

2. It is fine to let your team know that your preventative measures are in place to try to prevent job losses in the long term. (If there is an ultimatum and it is beyond your control, be honest and convey the urgency but not the threat.)

3. Respect your job, and respect all the people who help you get it done.

Reflection

- How did it work?

- What will I do next time?

References

Anderson, E. (2013) 21 quotes from Henry Ford on business, leadership and life, www.forbes.com, 31 May, http://www.forbes.com/sites/erikaandersen/2013/05/31/21-quotes-from-henry-ford-on-business-leadership-and-life/ (retrieved September 2015).

Cambridge Dictionary Online (2015) http://dictionary.cambridge.org/dictionary/english/false-economy (retrieved September 2015).

7.4 Being responsible

'The knowledge that we are responsible for our actions and attitudes does not need to be discouraging because it also means that we are free to change this destiny.'

(Anaïs Nin, 1969)

Why

Corporate social responsibility applies not only to you and your organisation but to those with whom you do business. Social media is quick to spread news about unethical practices (whether founded or not), and if you are unable to dispel the myths, your reputation will be tarnished. From carbon footprint to discrimination, the bigger the organisation the harder you can fall . . . and the more people there will be who may want to push you off your perch. High standards in these practices are easier to enforce locally, but they are also important if you outsource.

Business brief

Cost-saving outsourcing practices have been under scrutiny in the fashion industry, with Nike's link to sweatshops nearly costing them through public boycotts (Kokemuller, 2015). Apple, too, recently suffered a blip in their fortunes when it was found in 2010 that 18 members of the factory in China that made most of Apple's goods attempted suicide due to working practices (14 succeeded) (Jefferies, 2014). The reality is that if you say to someone 'You can buy this phone for *n* pounds, and this ethically manufactured one for *nnnn* pounds' the customer's own integrity is likely to become questionable. However, this does not make it right to condone poor practice. Further, your competition – whether or not they are guilty themselves – may continue to add fuel to the flame.

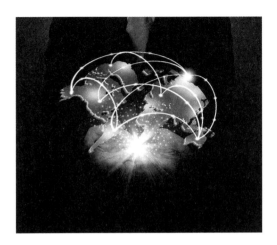

Try this

1. Be aware of the practices within your organisation – and those of your clients. If you outsource your work, ensure that the practices undertaken by the organisation in question comply with your own.

2. If you outsource, join the Ethical Trading Initiative, a UK-based company that since 1998 has been working to improve the lives of workers in global supply chains through their Code of Practice. The Code can be retrieved here: http://www.ethicaltrade.org/

3. Note that there is frequent debate on whether businesses should be promoting employment within their own country or outsourcing, and you may be asked to justify your choices.

4. Always be aware that you will only hear one side of any story, and sometimes it may not be accurate. Ethics is a sensitive area with huge repercussions if handled badly. If you are concerned, raise those issues internally first (following appropriate organisational protocol).

Reflection

- How did it work?

- What will I do next time?

References

Ethical Trading Initiative Code of Practice: http://www.ethicaltrade. org/eti-base-code (retrieved September 2015).

Jefferies, D. (2014) Is Apple cleaning up its act on labour rights? *The Guardian*, 5 March, http://www.theguardian.com/sustainable-business/apple-act-on-labour-right (retrieved September 2015).

Kokemuller, N. (2015) Is outsourcing an ethical practice? *Small Business Chronicle*, http://smallbusiness.chron.com/outsourcing-ethical-practice-80639.html (retrieved September 2015).

Nin, A. (1969) *The Diary of Anais Nin, Vol. 1: 1931–1934.* New York: Mariner Books.

7.5 Mad, bad, sad – treating a toxic organisation

'If personality were really the problem, the cure would be psychotherapy.'

(Chris Argryis, 1986)

Why

In the same way as a sick person finds it difficult to function, so too will a sick organisation. Companies, and on a smaller scale, departments, can become 'ill' due to the behaviour of those in charge. Do not let yours succumb.

Business brief

Robinson (2009) defined three areas of 'illness' within organisations and classified them as follows:

- Mad: 'odd, eccentric or dysfunctional patterns of thinking ... with reduced capacity for close interpersonal relationships'.
- Bad: 'impulsive or dramatic patterns of behaviour ... with a corresponding lack of empathy'.
- Sad: 'dependent, avoidant and obsessive compulsive ... disorders'.

Each of these types affect performance and organisational growth. Further, this organisational 'illness' sometimes either goes unrecognised because it is so embedded in practice or is ignored altogether (Frost, 2007).

If your behaviours, or those of any of your team or colleagues, give you any cause for concern, do not ignore the issue. Acknowledge and monitor the questionable behaviours to see whether a pattern emerges.

If you find that your organisation (or department) is sickly, Frost (2007) suggests the following:

- You may need to accept what you cannot change – but be aware that these patterns exist so that you can continue challenging them.

- You may decide to leave for a healthier workplace. (It is even possible – see section 3.6 on secondments – that you may return with ideas for ways in which you can treat the illness.)

Try this

This is a simple training exercise developed by Chris Argryis (1986) to uncover any prevailing 'sickly' routines. Do this exercise yourself or ask your team to do it.

1. Think of a relevant issue and write down what you would do about it.

2. Imagine you had the opportunity to bring the issue up at a meeting. On one half of a sheet of paper, write down what you would say.

3. On the other half of the paper, write down what you believe the response would be.

4. Now predict the outcome.

Argryis (1986) found that most people believed the response would be 'There's nothing we can do' or words to that effect, with most predicted outcomes being 'Save it for another meeting' – by which time the problem may have been forgotten or superseded.

If you find that the prediction and outcome are positive drivers for change, congratulations; if you find that yet another matter has been swept under the proverbial carpet, you may have a sickly organisation.

In this case:

- Examine the 'routines' identified by the exercise and see if you can address them individually, e.g. if someone says 'Nothing can be done' – ask the question anyway and follow it up with 'Why?'.

- If you can make a change – no matter how small – do it.

- Try not to let important issues go. Even if they cannot be solved at once, keep them as agenda points.

- Encourage your team to provide suggested solutions when they identify an issue – sometimes defensiveness is just a cover for not having any ideas.

- Consider the use of instilling creativity. While this is not to advocate GCSE Drama exercises, sometimes a meeting energiser which enables staff to be creative reminds them that 'no' does not always have to be an option:

  - *In one such exercise a team throws an imaginary ball to each other. As each person throws it, they say what it is. The receiver catches the ball and acknowledges what it is, then throws it on to another person, describing it as something else. This serves the purpose of developing creativity, but also acknowledging and accepting other people's ideas – no matter how wacky.*

Reflection

- How did it work?

```



```

- What will I do next time?

```



```

References

Argryis, C. (1986) Skilled incompetence, *Harvard Business Review,* September, https://hbr.org/1986/09/skilled-incompetence (retrieved September 2015).

Frost, P.J. (2007) *Toxic Emotions at Work and What You Can Do About Them.* Boston, MA: Harvard Business School Press.

Robinson, D.A. (2009) *Pathologies and Wellness in Entrepreneurial Firms,* Epublications.bond.edu.au, http://epublications.bond.edu.au/business_pubs/67 (retrieved September 2015).

7.6 Ethics in a globalised world

'Never doubt that a small group of thoughtful, committed citizens can change the world; indeed it's the only thing that ever has.'

(Margaret Mead, cited in Cool, 2008)

Why

Desensitisation can occur when you are constantly exposed to something which at first repulses you. Similarly, an unethical practice may at first appal, but as it becomes part of your everyday understanding of the world, it is easy to ignore. A business in the UK is able to deal with a business in a different part of the world where legal practices and sanctions may differ and so gain an advantage in terms of productivity. However, this is likely to come at a cost. Just because you may not see the impact directly, it does not mean that it is not happening. It is important to continue to remain, and keep those with whom you do business, accountable on ethical issues.

Business brief

Aslanman (2015) observed that with globalisation comes greater interdependence and integration, *and* a need for greater regulation surrounding trade. Rather than canny investments alone, globalisation offers organisations the opportunity to be educators and enforcers of basic rights for workers.

Ethical practice also applies to your own staff. 'Family Hold Back' (Collinson, 1927) – the practice where the guest (or in the business sense, the customer/client) always comes first, can be detrimental to organisational health. Of course the ultimate goal of a business is profit (as this ensures survival), but a rich organisation with no-one to run it is going to fail just as quickly.

Try this

1. Be explicit with your standards of ethical practice and expect the same from others with whom you work – whether they are clients, customers or employees.

2. If there is a practice you are unsure about, try to understand it from the point of view of the other person or business, and in turn request that they consider yours.

3. If an agreement cannot be reached, if your standards are explicit and a breach is clear, you should maintain your own standards whatever the consequences.

4. Appreciate that ethical decisions are not always clear cut.

5. Encourage your team to make ethical decisions themselves.

6. Be aware of, and implement, changes in ethical guidelines in industry standards.

7. Reflect regularly on your practice to ensure that you are not making your own employees sacrifice too much for the sake of profit.

Reflection

- How did it work?

```

```

- What will I do next time?

```

```

References

Aslanman, S. (2015) Gaps of social justice in a globalised world, paper presented at the International Journal of Arts and Sciences Conference, Las Vegas, 2015.

Collinson, W.E. (1927) *Contemporary English: A Personal Speech Record.* Berlin: B.G. Teubner.

Cool, J.C. (2008) *Communities of Innovation: Cyborganic and the Birth of Networked Social Media.* Ann Arbor, MI: ProQuest.

7.7 Be proactive

'The most dangerous phrase is "We've always done it this way".'
(Grace Hopper, cited in Johnson Lewis, 2015)

Why

Part of the purpose of this book is to think about your own practices. If you can understand why you behave in certain ways you will have a better understanding of at least one person in your organisation. You may also gain an insight into how others think and behave through observation, reflection and knowing that there are alternatives to every action. Once you have that understanding, what happens next is up to you. You can choose to make changes, or to keep things as they are, but a broadened insight means you remain in control. Management is not an easy ride, neither is it a clear road. You will need to make many judgment calls and your integrity will be tested. You may need to question your beliefs and your practices and sometimes make changes or exceptions. What is most important is that you remain proactive. Management is not a passive word, neither is it reactive. Being in charge means being able to shape your ride.

Business brief

Once someone has become 'institutionalised' they have become part 'of a particular system, society or organisation' (Cambridge Dictionary Online, 2015). This means that questionable practices are often not called to account, nor even recognised! The great manager remains aware of their own good practice as well as that of their team and colleagues, while knowing they can all always learn and evolve. Learning requires reflection on what has gone before, and then making changes which are continually modified as one acquires experience. According to Argryis and Schon (1978) many organisations excel at 'single loop' learning, which is responding to an incident (often) in the same way that they have always done – this may result in a short-term 'fix', but it does not allow the organisation to progress. For Argryis and Schon (1978) the only effective learning is 'double loop' – where assumptions and actions are constantly reviewed following reflection and new experiences. What often stands in the way of this sort of learning is pride, which leads to defensive behaviour. It is important to remember that business is about growth and sustainability – if you are not learning, you are not moving; if you are not moving, you are stagnating.

Make reflection and revision part of your ritual. You chose your role, you chose this book – you must be choosing to grow!

Try this

1. If someone questions a practice, try to look at it from their point of view. They may have identified a genuine flaw, or you may not have explained it correctly – both need your attention.

2. In responding to a problem, examine your assumptions critically – if they are unfounded, change them.

3. Reflect on your solutions and be realistic in your appraisal.

4. Do not be afraid of getting it wrong – that is the best way to learn. Remember, if you are not learning, you may be stagnating.

5. ALWAYS conduct an exit interview, whether in person or via an electronic platform. Too often people may choose to leave rather than question practices they believe cannot – or will not – change. Asking direct questions may give you some answers, and ideas for improvement. For example:

   (a) What changes in practice might you suggest to improve performance?

   (b) What do you feel we could have done better?

   (c) What could we have done to retain you?

Reflection

- How did it work?

- What will I do next time?

References

Argryis, C. and Schon, D. (1978) *Organizational Learning: A Theory of Action Perspective.* Reading, MA: Addison-Wesley.

Cambridge Dictionary Online (2015) http://dictionary.cambridge.org/dictionary/english/institutionalize (retrieved September 2015).

Johnson Lewis, J. (2015) *Women's History,* abouteducation.com, http://womenshistory.about.com/od/quotes/a/grace_hopper.htm (retrieved September 2015).

A note on case studies

All case study quotes within each chapter were collected during the author's PhD research published here: http://dspace.brunel. ac.uk/handle/2438/7038 (retrieved September 2015). Permission was given to use each example, with job title identification, and interviews were conducted pursuant to Brunel University's ethical permissions.

Index

Index

Index

team members, motivations of
   extrinsic 116, 119
   intrinsic 108, 120
   theories of 114

National Health Service (NHS) 212, 215
negativity 113, 120, 129, 132, 142, 213
negotiation 146
Neurolinguistic Programming (NLP) 16
Nike 218
Nin, A. 218

objectivity 59
observing 32, 126, 228
Ogilvy, D. 63
opportunities 9, 32, 50, 53, 75–6, 88,
     98–9, 103, 108, 124, 143, 145,
     166, 171, 177, 222, 225
organisational boundaries 11, 154
organisational grapevine, the *see* gossip
organisations 8, 29, 71, 99, 143, 198,
     225, 229
  attitudes towards 71
  cultures of 31, 98, 174, 189,
     205–207, 210–11, 213
  growth/development of 32, 64–5,
     95–6, 100, 209, 211–13, 216, 221
  missions and goals of 7, 12, 25,
     39–40, 46, 80–1, 89, 96, 125
  and their people 119, 202–203, 205,
     207, 214, 228
  policies and procedures of 4, 15, 19,
     42, 58–9, 81, 116, 175, 183, 187,
     211, 226
  strategy of 75, 211–13, 216, 228
  success of 38, 96, 203, 216, 218
  toxic 204–205, 213, 221–3
  understanding 98, 228
  values of 12, 107, 201, 204, 206,
     209–11, 218–19, 225–6
  view of 7
  vision of 8, 49, 64, 66, 107, 209
  well-being of 202–205, 213, 216, 222
outsourcing 96, 218–19, 225
over-familiarity 103
over-thinking 197

Parsons, L.C. 153
passion 108–109

Patton, B. 186
pay 116, 202, 212
people-focus 24
perceptions 88–9, 103, 123, 126, 180,
     195, 211
performance 8, 12, 46, 48, 71, 75, 80,
     84, 86, 95–7, 109, 114, 117–18,
     120, 122–3, 149, 155, 187, 201,
     203, 210, 221, 230
  improvements in 118, 214
  reviews of *see* appraisals
personal growth 43, 76, 86, 89, 93, 149,
     229
personal needs 38–9, 79
personality 21, 32, 99, 221
  inventories 48–9
perspective 7, 13, 28, 64, 77, 138 *see
     also* 'big picture'
planning 153
policies *see under* organisations
practices 4, 16, 19, 96, 201, 205, 207,
     218–19, 222, 226, 228–30
     see also Standard Operating
     Procedures (SOPs)
  departmental 19, 76
praise 30, 43, 52–3, 61–2, 88, 108,
     114–18, 143, 165–6, 188
predecessors 19
preferences 39, 48, 180
preparation 90
pressure 120
proactivity 8–9, 31, 65, 156, 228
probationary period *see* 'honeymoon
     period'
problems (at work) 60, 112, 120, 181,
     187, 221–2 *see also* teams,
     problems within/dysfunctional
  solving 151, 153, 160, 180–1, 230
     see also solutions
procedures 16 *see also* Standard
     Operating Procedures (SOPs)
productivity 46, 48, 108, 111
professionalism 26, 103, 184
profit 202, 225–6
progress 61, 74, 93, 107–108, 140, 214
projects 125
promises 26, 82
promotion 12, 94
publicity 195–6

238